Focus on Feathers

A Complete Guide to American Indian Feather Craft

by
J. Andrew Forsythe

D1614052

Published by Crazy Crow Trading Post

Packing Stone (Henry Tsoodle), Kiowa
Dressed in classic Southern Plains attire, his outfit consists of tab leggings with garters, fringe and gourd stitched tassels, buckskin shirt and leggings decorated with mescal beans and twisted fringe, large otter braid wraps, beaded braid ties with metallic fringe, a rolled neckerchief with a German silver "sunburst" tie slide, red broadcloth blanket, and he holds a loose, eagle fan. The fan contains at least ten immature black & white eagle tail feathers, with unusually large white markings on their tips. *McKee-Reddick Photo Collection.*

Published by: Crazy Crow Trading Post

Written and Illustrated by: Andrew Forsythe

Cover Design by: Michael Catellier

Designed by: Michael Catellier and J. Rex Reddick

Graphic Designer: Michael Catellier

Photographs by: Andrew Forsythe, Mike Reed, Earl Fenner, Mike Catellier, J. Rex Reddick, Ginger Otipoby Reddick,

John Butler and C. Scott Evans

ISBN 1-929572-13-1

Table of Contents

Forward

For individuals engaged in any type of craftwork today, information on both instructions and materials is generally readily available. Those who specifically make American Indian crafts can search and find many materials available to them from various suppliers, especially using the Internet. Some specific craft materials that were only available in the past are now being reproduced once again. These fine reproductions include such items as seed beads in historic colors, correct-looking trade cloths, and resin casts of various bone and other animal parts, just to name a few. Probably one of the most noticed items associated with American Indian crafts is the feather. While entire industries are actively involved in supplying the general marketplace with various feathers of all kinds, the feathers often associated with American Indian craftwork are those from raptors or, as they are more commonly referred to, birds of prey.

For many years, feather companies have offered their own versions of imitation raptor feathers, generally being mass produced by the available techniques common to the industry. Using the standard that is still being employed today, these feathers gave the craftworker an essential item at an economical cost. It is no fault of the feather supply houses that these imitations have for decades remained unchanged. Never mind what they look like, the price is right!

In recent years, demand for a more realistic imitation raptor feather has come from those working in American Indian crafts. This specific type of product, however, is generally in short supply when compared to the other reproduction craft materials available to the craftworker. With all the technology available to us today, it would probably be easier for one to re-create an extinct dinosaur raptor than a present-day feathered raptor!

For many supply houses, feathers for American Indian crafts remain only a small part of their market. Creating 'realistic' imitations of birds of prey feathers for the marketplace may or may not be within their scope of resources or capabilities. Confronting this situation has been one reason for creating this book.

Today, only a handful of dedicated individuals are actively involved in providing specific raptor feather reproductions. Andy Forsythe is one of these individuals. Those who have created their own imitations of raptor feathers have found the need to acquire a new set of craft skills. This process alone may be the leading factor in keeping a number of individuals from taking on this new experience. The steps outlined in the following pages are intended to make the procedure a little less frustrating and, as a result, more rewarding.

Andy's interest has gone beyond that of creating feather reproductions to that of studying the featherwork techniques employed in various American Indian crafts. His passion for feather knowledge has taken him to visit old resources and to find new ones. Through time, this information started to pile up! Given his professional background as a teacher and his enthusiasm over feather studies, the need to share this information was inevitable. With many specific books already on the market covering most of the major crafts of the American Indian, information on feathers had to be gleaned from multiple sources. This repository of information is designed to grow beyond what is being shown in the following pages. In addition to illustrating common techniques and practices employed in featherwork, new methods being used by today's featherworkers are also included.

For those who share this interest in American Indian featherwork, let these pages be a source of reference and a platform for future discussions. It is my hope that if the information presented in Andy's book can get one person interested in the field of creating feather reproductions, it will all be worthwhile!

I saw it happen once. This book is the result.

Robert W. Laidig

Acknowledgements

As any such endeavor of this kind is not the work of a sole individual, I would like to recognize those who have contributed their knowledge and support throughout this project.

Firstly, I give thanks to my Lord and Savior for all His blessings in my life and especially for the guidance and strength to see this project to fruition.

Great appreciation is expressed to my wife and daughter for their loving support and encouragement. My wife, Tricia, has been my sounding board each step of the way. Sabrina, I thank you for your patience and understanding each time I was unable to spend time with you due to the demands of my work schedule to keep on task for this book.

I would not know the success I have in my business of featherwork and subsequently, this book would not have come about without the tutelage and guidance of my friend and mentor, Bob Laidig. I am most grateful for all the advice and encouragement you have freely offered me over the years. You ignited the spark and fed the flames of my passion for this exciting art form. Thank you.

While I may have taken some time to compile the craft tips on featherwork into this one volume, I certainly cannot claim them all to be my own creative inventions. The following is a list of people who have unselfishly given of their time and knowledge and as such have contributed to the contents of this book. To each of them, I am most grateful.

Dana LaQuay, Craig Jones, Thom Meyers, Bob Patyk, Don Hockenberry, John Kursch, Mike Reed, Tom McClain, B.D., Earl Fenner, Jim Cooley, Barry Hardin, Members of the Plains, Prairie & Plateau e-group, Yale Peabody Museum, Barry Landua at American Museum of Natural History, Daisy Njoku at The Smithsonian Institution, and Charles Scott at the State Historical Society of Iowa.

I wish to say a special thank you to my brother Edo, who was my Editor-in-Chief. Your suggestions and revisions shaped this book into its finished form. Thank you for your patience and persistence.

Osage Dancers, 1920's or early 1930's
These dancers are wearing early style straight dance outfits and two of the men are carrying eagle tail fans, while another has a fan made of a hawk tail. The man on the far right is Wilson Kirk, a prominent Grayhorse Osage. Glass Negative Photo.

John Butler, Sac & Fox
John is wearing his fine, Northern Traditional outfit and carrying his eagle wing fan, staff and hoop, both of which have eagle tail feathers in varying colorations suspended from them. The bases of these feathers are wrapped with red wool cloth.
Photo courtesy of John Butler.

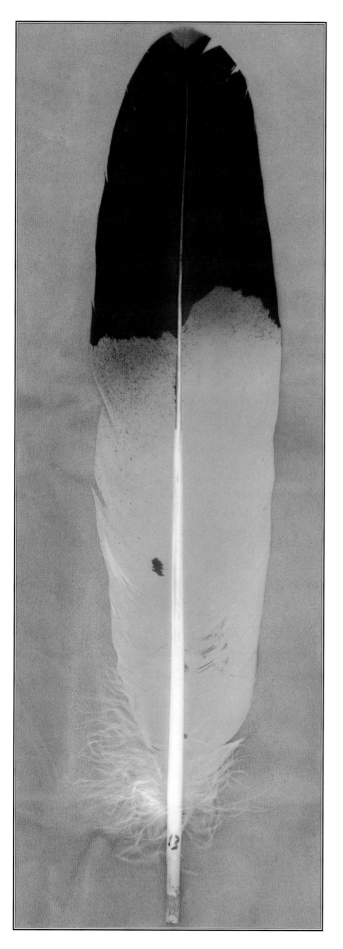

Chapter 1

Ornithology 101

This chapter will serve as your introduction to Ornithology, the study of birds. The goal is not the conversion of the masses into amateur ornithologists, but a development of appreciation of the structure and beauty of the birds' most unique characteristic, the feather. Just as sculptors must possess an intimate knowledge and understanding of the structure of the stone or clay with which they bring to life their visions, a feather-worker must develop a greater understanding of the feather and all its faculties, before it is employed within the creation of the crafter's work. It is upon this premise that this chapter rests.

While a number of individuals may consider themselves to be able-minded enough to differentiate between an eagle and a hawk feather, they find themselves at a loss when such a broad distinction no longer suffices. Indeed, many are surprised to learn of the existence of more than one type of eagle indigenous to North America and are generally hard-pressed to name more than three hawk species endemic to their region of North America. This should not be viewed as an indictment of the knowledge of Americans at large, but, if anything, a conviction of the educational system for having overlooked the most extraordinary line of creatures with whom we share this planet. The beauty in diversity, of the Class Aves, is beyond compare, and, in my opinion, a proof of Intelligent Design, for only God could conceive of something so remarkable in form and function.

Ornithology 101

This introduction to the study of ornithology will focus mainly on the topography of birds, the structure of feathers (see **Figure 1.1**) and the different types of feathers found on the bird. While there is a great deal more information to be uncovered by those who are ambitious enough to seek it, the topics mentioned herein will suffice to educate the novice ornithologist of the basics required for our study of featherwork.

Figure 1.1 presents a wing feather and identifies the various parts of the feather. These will be referred to throughout the book so it would be useful to learn these parts. There is also a glossary of general avian terms at the end of this chapter. Leading edge and trailing edge are terms used when referring to wing (remiges) or tail (retrices) feathers only and not the contour or covert feathers of the body because it is only the main wing and tail feathers that are involved in the creation of lift for flight. Each flight feather is an airfoil with the leading edge curved slightly higher than the trailing edge so that the overall shape of the feather is a curve. This causes the air molecules to pass over the dorsal surface faster which reduces downward forces on the top of the feather and results in lift, or the upward force on the bottom of the feather.

So, as each feather gains lift and the entire wing is also an airfoil with a curved top and concave bottom the entire wing has lift as it glides through the air and the entire bird can fly. Since the body feathers aren't used for lift for flight we don't distinguish a leading and trailing edge on those feathers.

Please note that the stiff central shaft of a feather is known as a rachis, not quill. I use this term repeatedly throughout the book when discussing feather alterations and usages. While quill is used in common parlance for the rachis of a feather, I use the term quill only when specifically referring to the lower, hollow shaft of a feather. This hollow shaft is also known as the calamus and I also use that term repeatedly so that you know exactly which part of the feather I'm referring to when presenting various techniques.

Figure 1.1

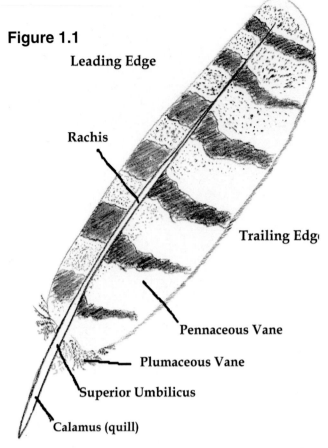

Leading Edge

Rachis

Trailing Edge

Pennaceous Vane

Plumaceous Vane

Superior Umbilicus

Calamus (quill)

As the previous paragraphs mention a few types of feathers found on birds let's look at these types more closely. There are four major categories of feathers to be considered. Several of these categories contain several varieties of feathers each possessing unique characteristics we will investigate later. The main categories are [refer to the sketches in **Figure 1.2**)

Contour feathers are feathers possessing a pennaceous vane such as body feathers, flight feathers of the wing and tail, and the various coverts of the wing and tail. Plumaceous barbs may be present at the superior umbilicus and as the aftershaft.

Semiplumes & down feathers consist entirely of plumaceous barbs which lack the hooklets or hamuli (see **Figure 1.3**) to form a pennaceous vane. Semiplumes have a more rigid rachis than down. Down is found throughout the body near the skin for protection and warmth. While all birds have down, some birds have more depending on their environmental conditions.

Bristles appear hair-like as they consist mostly of a rachis and may contain a small clustering of plumaceous barbs at the base of the feather. Often found around the eyes and lores of the face, these feathers act like whiskers on a cat providing sensory input.

Filoplumes are hair-like feathers with a bare rachis and small amount of plumaceous barbs near the tip. Filoplumes act as sensory perception of air flow around face, nape and wings. On some birds, the filoplume extends beyond the surface of the flight feathers in order to gauge wind speed and detect exact wing feather position during flight. Sensory corpuscles (known as Herbst corpuscles) around the base of the feather follicle allow the bird to detect the position of every feather.

While one can categorize feathers into these four general groups, the specific feathers on a bird can be further classified by distinguishing, structural characteristics and by their location on the body. The chart below presents each of these varieties of feathers.

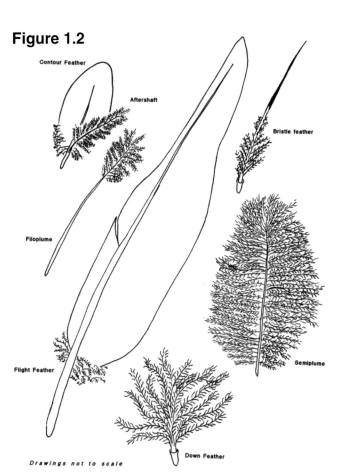

Figure 1.2

Adapted from Manual of Ornithology, Proctor & Lynch, 1993

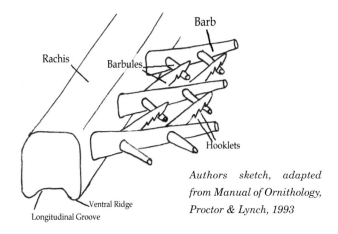

Authors sketch, adapted from Manual of Ornithology, Proctor & Lynch, 1993

Figure 1.3

This diagrammatic sketch shows how the hamuli (a.k.a. hooklets) of the distal barbules grab onto the proximal barbules adjacent to them. This forms the solid webbing of pennaceous vanes. Plumaceous vane barbules lack the hooklets necessary to join together the barbs to create a rigid structure. The process of barbules 'zipping up' the barbs of the feather is much like a zipper bringing together two sides of a coat or as Velcro pieces that can be pulled apart and then just as easily preened back together again.

Young Kiowa Boy
This young man is wearing a stand up style war bonnet with a simple brow band and ribbon side drops. His finery includes a war shirt, Southern Plains style short bone breastplate and a miniature peace medal suspended from a wide ribbon. *McKee-Reddick Photo Collection.*

Body Feathers

These small feathers found along the body in segmented tracts called pterylae cover the body for warmth and protection. Pennaceous vanes are symmetrical along the rachis with plumaceous vane at superior umbilicus. Aftershaft feather is often as long as the body feather.

Remiges

Flight feathers of the wing, consisting of primary, secondary and tertials. (see wing diagram Figure 1.4) Pennaceous vane is asymmetrical in primaries with the trailing edge wider than the leading edge. Secondaries and tertials are symmetrical. Aftershaft is shortened and often indistinguishable from plumaceous barbs.

Retrices

Large, vaned flight feathers of the tail. Similar in structure to the remiges. Retrices' vanes become increasingly asymmetrical towards the outer edge of the tail, with the trailing edge wider than the leading edge. Aftershaft is shortened and often indistinguishable from plumaceous barbs.

Alula

This wing feather group equates to the 'thumb' of the wing. Found along the leading edge as a cluster of 3-4 feathers that can be moved independently from the other remiges to adjust air flow over the wing in flight. Pennaceous vane is asymmetrical like other primary flight feathers. Also known as alular quills. (see wing diagram Figure 1.4)

Axillaries

Also known as wingpit feathers (as opposed to armpit) as they are found on the underside of the wing, near the point of attachment of the wing to the body. These are a specialized type of covert being more elongated than other secondary underwing coverts. Pennaceous vaned.

Coverts

These feathers lay in rows along the dorsal and ventral wing and tail near the point of attachment of the remiges and retrices respectively. Layered like shingles of a roof, these provide protection and help create the aerodynamic airfoil necessary for flight. Wings possess greater primary, greater secondary, lesser secondary, median and marginal (see Figure 1.4). Tail coverts are known as upper tail and under tail coverts. Under tail coverts are semiplumes with more plumaceous vane while all other coverts are pennaceous vaned

Figure 1.4

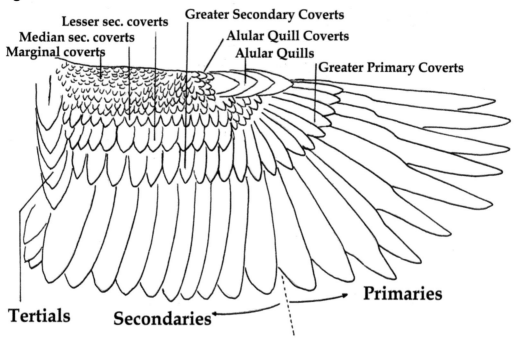

Authors sketch redrawn from Manual of Ornithology; Proctor & Lynch 1993

Before we discuss the process of creating imitation raptor feathers it is imperative that we investigate the true color and design of the raptor feathers we intend to imitate. There are those who are accomplished at identifying various raptors in flight or when alighted in a treetop but it's a different skill entirely to identify specific species of birds from a single feather. This skill is essential when studying the materials of the 18th, 19th and early 20th centuries as well as making note of particular feathers seen today. Most especially, it is this skill that must be cultivated when preparing to skillfully reproduce feathers for craftwork.

You must begin to see a feather in detail rather than the whole structure at once. Make note of the number of horizontal bars of a hawk's wing feather; the width of the bars of a Cooper's Hawk tail versus a Sharp-shinned Hawk tail; the color of the rachis along its entire length (dorsal & ventral view); the presence of light-shaded, detail markings; the round versus oblong style of mottling of a mature Golden Eagle tail feather; and so much more. Several of the reference photos have a thumbnail image next to the large image to emphasize this very point. The thumbnail view shows general design features that many associate with raptor feathers but the large image shows the actual details of each feather.

Details of the rachis, slight shades in hue, detail markings as spots and even negative spaces with no markings are only visible when you look closely at the large photo. As Bob Laidig used to point out to me, noting the details of the feather markings makes the difference between a 10 foot, 5 foot, and a 1 foot feather. He wasn't referring to a feather's size, rather, the distance at which an imitation feather reveals itself as an imitation. A ten foot feather may have the general appearance of an eagle feather from a distance so it will look quite realistic from across a dance arbor but as soon as one gets just ten feet away you can discern the inaccuracies that reveal it to be a faux raptor feather. As the result of Bob's tutelage my goal in raptor reproductions has been to produce a one foot feather, a feather of such exacting detail that it only becomes apparent that it's a reproduction when you hold it in your hand.

Right: Rusty & Dusty Wahkinney, Comanche. Dusty enjoys performing a War Dance as his dad, Rusty, sings for him. Photo taken in the early 1970's.

McKee-Reddick Photo Collection.

In the next chapter, **Reproducing Raptor Feathers,** I present several key characteristics in structure and design but it is important that you develop your own eye for detail. As you flip through the reference photos make note of the details you see in each of the images.

Special Note

As an introduction to the reference photos that follow I should perhaps make certain points clear regarding the subject matter of these photos. The photos throughout the reference section and the rest of the book are from my collection of photos unless otherwise noted. I take photos of feathers while traveling to pow-wows around the country. I often ask perfect strangers if I can photograph their feathers. Museums and university ornithological collections are an excellent resource for accessing feathers and taking detail photographs of those feathers. Many long hours were spent studying raptor feathers in the Juniata College ornithological collection during my years of study there. The photos provided by Mr. Fenner were obtained in the same manner decades ago, in an ornithological collection. Several of the reference photos herein were taken at Montour Preserve, a small educational center near my home. All this is mentioned to clarify that I do not use or traffic in protected feathers. One does not need to possess such feathers to study them intimately.

Glossary of Avian Terminology

Accipitridae – taxonomic classification of the Family of raptors, consisting of eagles, hawks, osprey, kites and harriers.

Accipiter – taxonomic classification of genus of hawks characterized by narrow, pointed wings and long, slender tails. Genus includes Sharp-shinned hawk Accipiter striatus, Cooper's hawk Accipiter cooperi

Aftershaft – A diminutive, secondary feather attached to the main feather at the superior umbilicus of the ventral side of the feather. See **Figure 1.2,** contour feather.

Alula a.k.a. alular quills – group of flight feathers attached to the first digit of the hand. Usually 3-4 feather group collectively known as alular quills. The alular quills lay along the front edge of the wing.

Anal circlet – the fold of skin forming the anus, found under the base of the tail

Apteria – see Pterylosis.

Axillaries – elongated covert feathers of the underwing found near the point of attachment of the wing to the body, a.k.a. wingpit feathers.

Barb – make up the feather's pennaceous and plumaceous vanes, these extend from either side of the rachis parallel to each other. See **Figure 1.3**.

Buteo – taxonomic classification of Genus of most broad-winged raptors characterized by rounded wing tips; broad, flat wings; and short, rounded tails. Genus includes such hawks as Red-tailed (Buteo jamaicensis), Red-shouldered (Buteo lineatus), Ferruginous (Buteo regalis), Broad-winged (Buteo platypterus), and Rough-legged (Buteo lagopus), among others.

Barbules – extensions branching off either side of the barbules and contain the hamuli that grab adjacent barbules to form the feather's vane. See **Figure 1.3**.

Calamus (quill) – the hardened, hollow shaft of the rachis that inserts into the bird for attachment. This region of the feather does not contain vanes.

Contour Feather – include any of the body and flight feathers with pennaceous vane.

Coverts - varieties include greater primary, greater secondary, median secondary, lesser secondary and marginal coverts on the wing and upper and under tail coverts of the tail.

Diastataxic feather configuration – wing configuration in which the 5th secondary flight feather is absent leaving a diastema, noticeable only by the presence of an extra underwing, greater secondary covert feather. Most members of the Accipitridae family have this wing configuration. See also Eutaxic feather configuration.

Dorsal – the upper or 'top' side of a bird or any part of a bird, e.g. parts of the bird or feathers that would be facing the sun when the bird is soaring.

Down feather – small feathers located close to the skin and contain only plumaceous vanes, often lacking a central rachis. These provide warmth and protection and are found most abundantly on waterfowl.

Emarginate primaries – primary remiges with a noticeably slender tip, distinctive notch on each vane and wider vane on the lower portion of the feather. Various Buteos, vultures, falcons and crows possess such primary wings which gives an image of fingers splayed wide when the birds are viewed in flight. This structure aides in flight as each feather gains lift as air passes between the primary feathers. See **Figure 1.4**.

Eutaxic feather configuration – a wing that contains one secondary covert feather for each of the secondary remiges. See also Diastataxic feather configuration.

Falconidae – taxonomic classification of Family within the order Falconiformes, consisting of falcons.

Hooklet, a.k.a. Hamuli – curved hooks along the distal barbules of a barb which grab the proximal barbules of the adjacent barbs to form a pennaceous vane of a contour feather. **See Figure 1.3**.

Inferior umbilicus – the tip of the calamus (quill) where the feather was attached to the bird.

Leading edge a.k.a. anterior vane – on asymmetrical flight feathers the thinner vane is the leading edge. See **Figure 1.1**.

Longitudinal groove - the indented groove that runs along the length of the ventral (bottom) side of the rachis. Most notable on the main flight feathers of the wing and tail. See **Figure 1.3**.

Lore – region of the bird's head between the beak and eye.

Nape – the back of the head and neck region

Natal Down – set of down feathers that are on baby birds for protection and warmth. Vary slightly in structure from down of adult birds.

Ornithology – the scientific study of birds, including recreational birdwatching

Pennaceous vane – flexible webbing of a contour feather that is created by the connections between the barbs of the vane in which the barbules grasp each other to form a solid vane. See **Figures 1.1 & 1.2**.

Plumaceous vane – barbs lacking the barbules with hamuli necessary for forming solid vanes. Plumaceous vanes are found on most feather types to some degree with the down feather being exclusively plumaceous vane. See **Figures 1.1 & 1.2**.

Powder Down – type of down feather whose unique characteristic is in the breakage of barbules into fine powder, thought to help with waterproofing.

Primaries (primary remiges) – major flight feathers of the wing and are attached to the skeletal bones that would be considered the 'hand'. Raptors generally have 10 primary remiges which have asymmetrical pennaceous vanes. See **Figure 1.4**. See also emarginate primaries.

Pterylosis, also pterylae – the pattern of distribution of feathers over a birds' body. The regional tracts where feathers are attached in clusters or groups are known as pterylae (singular, pteryla). These feathered regions are separated by areas lacking feathers known as apteria (singular, apterium).

Rachis – the central, stiff shaft to which the barbs attach much like the trunk of a tree which sprout limbs. Commonly referred to as the 'quill'. Remiges (singular Remex) consist of primary and secondary flight feathers. Also known as pinion feathers. See also Primaries and Secondaries. Retrices (singular Rectrix) main flight feathers of the tail. Members of the family Accipitridae generally have 12 or 14 retrices. Feathers attached nearer the center of the tail have symmetrical vanes along the central rachis while feathers nearer the outside edges have asymmetrical vanes with the leading edge being the thinner vane.

Rump – dorsal region of the body at the base of the tail.

Secondaries (secondary remiges) – major flight feathers attached to the ulna of the forearm. These feathers make up the main airfoil of the wing for flight and generally possess symmetrical vanes along the rachis helping to distinguish them from the primaries. See **Figure 1.4**.

Scapulars – feather group located on the dorsal area at the point of attachment of the wing. This feather group is part of a pteryla just over the scapula of the skeletal structure.

Superior umbilicus – region of a feather where the aftershaft is connected on the ventral side of the rachis. See **Figure 1.1**.

Tegmen layer - the thickened vane portion lying along the rachis of primary remiges of waterfowl. This strengthening structure is not found on raptors and may be used as a method of determining species of origin of individual feathers.

Tertiaries (Tertials) – feather group of the dorsal wing located near the body. These are larger than the greater secondary coverts they lay next to but are not part of this feather row nor of the secondary coverts. See **Figure 1.4**.

Trailing edge a.k.a. posterior vane – on asymmetrical flight feathers, the wider vane is the trailing edge. See **Figure 1.1**.

Uropygial gland - oily gland located on the rump at the base of the tail. Birds gather oils from this gland when preening feathers.

Vane – flexible webbing on either side of the stiff, central shaft (rachis) of a feather.

Ventral - the underside of a bird or parts of a bird, e.g. the parts of the bird or feathers that would be facing the ground when a bird is soaring.

Ventral Ridge – lay along either side of the longitudinal groove of the ventral side of the rachis. See **Figure 1.3**.

John Butler, Sac & Fox
This photo of John's Northern Tradtional bustle shows the fine detail in the feather work and decorations as well as the beautifully matched black and white eagle tail feathers. *Photo courtesy of John Butler.*

14

These photos are good representatives of immature Golden Eagles. Notice the added spotting on the bottom set of photos and the light color on the tips of several fethers in both tail sets. These sets are first year plumage of females. *R. J. Voelker collection; photos by Earl Fenner.*

R. J. Voelker Collection.
Photos by Earl Fenner.

Second year plumage of Golden Eagle. Small detail spots become larger as the beginnings of the barring indicative of mature eagles develop.

Third year plumage of Golden Eagle. The barring of mature feathers become more pronounced on the upper half of feathers. The dark tip extends farther down the feather before mottling begins.

Fourth year plumage of Golden Eagle. The barring continues to increase as the feathers mature and it now covers more than half of the upper part of the feathers.

Mature Golden Eagle feathers with only a small amount of white remaining at their bases and interspersed through the lower two-thirds of the feather.

R. J. Voelker Collection.
Photos by Earl Fenner.

Adult male Golden Eagle, 5+ years old.

Thumbnail photos are included to emphasize the need for noting details as opposed to abstract markings.

Bustle set made entirely of mature Golden Eagle tail feathers.

Golden Eagle secondary and tertial wing feathers.

Immature Bald Eagle, 2-3 years old bird. Note the axillary, underwing and undertail coverts as well as the secondary wing feathers of this young bird.

Two immature Bald Eagle fan sets. First year plumage is shown to the right. Second year plumage to the left. *M. Reed Photos*

Bald Eagle axillary Feather, juvenile.

Left: Front and back view of mature Golden Eagle fan set. Notice also the tail coverts.

Above: Mature Golden Eagle roach feather.

Northern Harrier (Marsh Hawk)
Left: Adult Male

Below: Adult Female

*All photos courtesy of the R. J. Voelker Collection;
photos by Earl Fenner.*

Harrier Hawk
Right: Adult

Red
Shouldered Hawk
Below: Adult

Swainson's Hawk
Above: Adult

Below: Juvenile

Merlin
Right: Adult

Northern Goshawk

Left:
Immiture, Female

Right:
Mature, Male

Rough-Legged Hawk

Right: Immiture

Below: Mature

Cooper's Hawk

Right:
Mature, Female

Red-Tailed Hawk

Left: Immiture, both males and femails exhibit the banded feathers for several years.

Above: Mature. Mature birds will most likely retain only the one bar near the end but Western birds may retain some faint bars along the feather.

*All photos on ths page
courtesy of Earl Fenner*

20

Harlan's Red-Tail Hawk

Below Left: Mature
Below Right: Immature, 1st Plumage
R. J. Voelker Collection; Earl Fenner Photo

Ferruginous Hawk

Left: Immature, 1st Plumage
Below: Adult
R. J. Voelker Collection; Earl Fenner Photo

Red-Tail Hawk

Below: Mature tail set and misc, wing feathers on bustle trailer.

M.Reed Photo

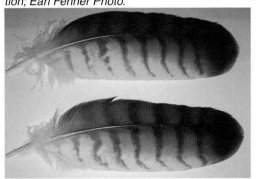

Osprey, Mature tail. *R. J. Voelker Collection; Earl Fenner Photo.*

Red-Tail Hawk Wing Feathers

Above: Trailer

Left: Secondaries

Rough Led Hawk Wing

Red Shoulder Hawk Wing

Red-Tail Hawk

Left: Primary wing feathers. Note also the primary coverts and alular quills.

Right: Secondaries flight feathers.

Great Horned Owl

Clockwise From Above:
Primary, Secondary, and Tertal Wing, Tail Feather, and the full wing with coverts.

Yellow-Shafted Flicker

Above: Top and bottom view of tail feathers
Below: Secondary wing feathers.

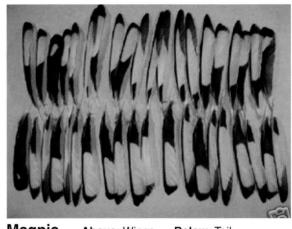

Magpie   **Above:** Wings   **Below:** Tail

Yellow-Shafted Flicker

Left: Secondary wing feathers.

Kestrel, Female

Right: Tail
Below:
Wing, underside.

Scissortail Tail Feathers

Kestrel, male

Left: Top two feathers are tail, uppermost is the outer edge feather. Bottom two are wing feathers.

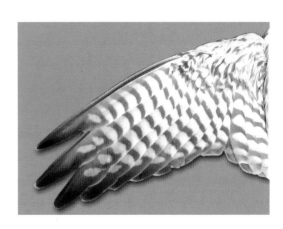

23

Red Cloud, *Sioux Chief*   *McKee-Reddick Photo Collection.*

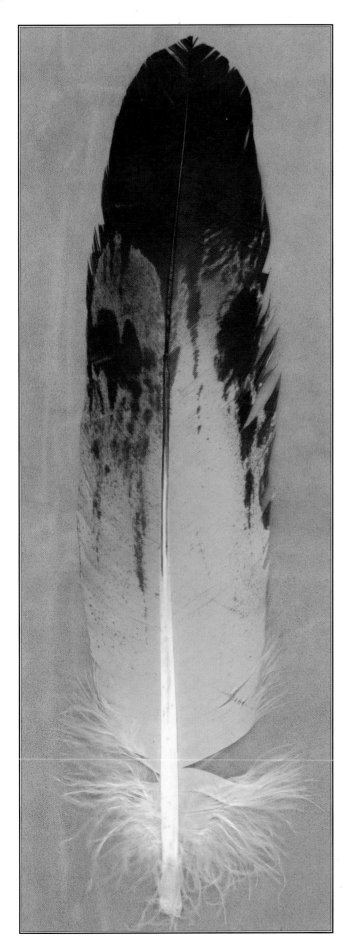

Chapter 2

Reproducing Raptor Feathers

*P*roducing a realistic raptor feather is a multi-step process. I will endeavor to lay out the following chapter in the order of steps I follow in the production of raptor feathers.

Chapter 1 is actually the first step of the process, reference materials to know what a real raptor feather looks like. Please study Chapter 1 at length, as well as accumulating your own reference photos of the feathers you wish to reproduce, before attempting to paint your own feathers. By planning your work well, with a very clear goal of the type of feather you wish to produce, you will increase your chances of success.

For the purpose of elucidating the process of painting a feather, we will begin by walking through the steps for reproducing the immature Golden Eagle tail feather, as it is the most widely recognized, and most often utilized, in dance outfits and craftwork.

Selecting Feathers

The basic canvas used by feather painters is the white, domestic turkey wing feather. These can be purchased in bulk quantities, by the pound from a variety of suppliers. If your goal is to produce a few feathers for yourself, and perhaps for your friends, then I suggest that you purchase the 'Select' or 'Jumbo' white feathers, available from a craft supplier.

These have already been pre-sorted, to find the longest and widest feathers, which more closely resemble the size of a real eagle feather. While the per-feather cost is higher than purchasing by the pound, you are more likely to get a greater number of usable feathers for eagle tails.

Of course, don't throw away the thinner feathers, as they are needed for hawk and owl feathers. When you receive your feathers, begin by sorting them into categories of use; e.g. eagle tails, eagle wings, hawk and owl, etc.

Straightening Feathers

Once you have your feathers sorted, prepare them by straightening first. Turkey wings don't have the same three-dimensional shape as a raptor tail feather, shaping them is the first stage to creating the illusion of a raptor feather. Along with the illusionary effect, the straight feather is easier to paint on, instead of trying to straighten it after it has been painted.

There are several methods one can employ in straightening a feather. The easiest and the one least likely to damage the feathers is direct steam, from an iron. While holding the feather on the ironing surface, lightly pass the steaming iron over the feather. DO NOT TOUCH THE FEATHER. The hot steam will cause the rachis to soften from its natural curve and allow you to bend it in the opposite direction of the natural curve. Once you have the feather flexed, from the hot steam, remove the heat and allow the feather to cool. Holding the feather bent in the opposite direction of its natural curve while it cools will cause it to stay straight. Take your time on this technique so as to avoid scorching the feathers or yourself. Practice on the 'seconds' you set aside while sorting.

Another benefit to the use of steam is the preening of the webbing. The hot steam helps the rumpled and frayed feather vanes go back into place for a better looking feather. Use your fingers to gently stroke the webbing while it is still warm from the steam, to restore the vane to its original shape.

Another method utilizes the dry heat of a bare light bulb to coerce the rachis into the straightened position. Be sure to wear the very darkest sunglasses you can find, while attempting this technique. Gently rub the hot bulb along the rachis with one hand, as you use the other to straighten the rachis. You can use just the tip of your iron in the same fashion as the light bulb. Turn the iron to a setting lower than steam so it's not too hot and gently work your way along the rachis.

These methods take much longer as you only heat a short section of the rachis at a time but the dry heat works better for setting the rachis in a more permanent position. Steamed feathers are more susceptible to high humidity. After a long weekend of dancing in the humid air of late spring, your painted eagle feathers may begin to curve like turkey wings again.

Preparing the Rachis

Under close scrutiny, one can observe the shiny, protective film along the length of the rachis. You need to remove this layer of protective protein before painting the feather. Once removed, the paints can adhere to the rachis better. The edge of a scissor held perpendicular to the rachis will easily shave off the material in long curls. (**Figure 2.1**) Again, practice on the smaller feathers so as to avoid damaging your premium feathers. Do both the front and back of the feather.

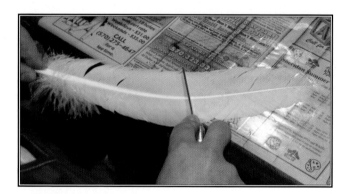

Figure 2.1
Scraping the rachis to remove shiny coating.

Painting the Feather

The first step, in the actual painting, is to refer back to your reference photos. Surround yourself with photos of the types of feathers you wish to paint and refer to them often when you have a brush in hand.

The paints, or dyes, one can use, are many and varied, but, it doesn't matter what you use so long as you make a realistic feather. Acrylic paints are often used, a mixture of dark umber and burnt sienna. Thin your paints with rubbing alcohol as water-based materials will only bead up on the feather rather than soak in. Other dyes and paints worth trying are silk, feather, leather and fur dyes, oil paints, or wood stains. For the immature Golden Eagle tail feathers we're producing, we want a deep, dark brown, not necessarily black. While the youngest of eagles seem to have a black tip, closer inspection reveals it to be the darkest of brown.

Purchase several squirrelette brushes of varying sizes. A soft-bristled brush is important so that the bristles gently flow the paint onto the feather without separating the vane barbules.

Once you have your paints, a selection of brushes, paper towels and a work area that can withstand a little mess, you're ready to paint. (See **Figure 2.2**) With the feather laid out flat in front of you, paint one side at a time. I use an old sad-iron to hold the feather down, thus keeping my hands free. On the leading edge, the dark color comes down farther on the webbing. (See **Figure 2.3**)

Figure 2.3
Painting leading edge

There is a lot of variation from one eagle to the next, but, generally speaking, the leading edge comes down farther along the rachis on feathers farther from the center of the tail. As I've mentioned before, there is no 'center' feather but the two in the middle often have a leading edge and trailing edge that nearly match each other. Paint in short strokes with the grain of the webbing, from the center to the edge, applying an even coat of paint. Pick a reference photo to determine how you want to finish the bottom of the dark section with a swirl or dip or spots and speckles.

When finished on the first side, move over to the trailing edge. (**Figure 2.4**) This side does not come down all the way to match the leading edge. Once again, there is certainly a lot of variation among real feathers, so, refer to your reference photos for ideas of how to finish off the bottom of the dark section

Figure 2.2
This is my work area. Reference photos surround me. On the left are white feathers ready to paint and on the right is my drying rack. The painting surface is newspaper laminated with clear packing tape.

Figure 2.4
Painting trailing edge

Use a fine-tipped brush to add detail markings below where the color ends. (**Figure 2.5**) I apply detail markings in as many as four layers. I hand-stipple detail spots and specks with a fine-tipped brush, then, spritz on other layers of specks with a toothbrush. Tear a hole in a paper towel and flick the bristles of the toothbrush, with your thumb, to spritz paint onto the feather. The hole will guide just where you want the paint spots to go. (See **Figure 2.6**) I also lay two paper towel edges together in a V, or along one side of the rachis, to direct the paint spatters. I don't want it to look haphazard and carefree, but, deliberate and intentional, as if those spots are there in that particular pattern because that's exactly what I saw in the reference photo. Take your time on the detail markings. Not all feathers have a lot of detail markings, while others have a lot. Check your reference photo often and scrutinize it carefully for the details as you transfer those details onto your feather.

Figure 2.5   Hand-stippling with fine brush

Before setting this feather aside to dry, use your medium or fine-tip brush to carefully paint the rachis to a point just below where the main color ends, on the leading edge. Flip the feather over to paint the rachis of the underside of the feather. Do not lay the feather down to do this, but hold the feather in one hand while lightly brushing over the rachis.

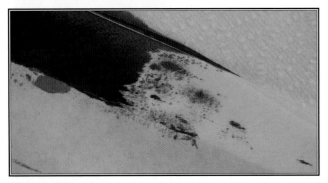

Figure 2.6   Spritzing detail prior to overspray. Paper towel guides the paint.

When you're finished painting, set your feather aside to dry and prepare for the next one. An old box with holes poked through or piece of styrofoam will serve as a drying rack. Depending on your choice of paint or dye it may be necessary to paint the feather in several thin layers. Applying multiple, thin layers of a lighter color can sometimes result in a better looking feather than if you slather on a thick layer of paint in one stroke. If you need to or choose to do several layers of paint, allow sufficient drying time between applications, before moving on to the finishing steps.

Use an airbrush to layer on a light color along the bottom edge of the painted sections of the feather. (**Figure 2.7**) You can use the same paint you used before and thin it with rubbing alcohol to flow

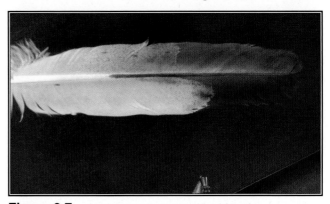

Figure 2.7   Applying overspray with airbrush.

through the sprayer better and give you a lighter color that will help transition from the dark top to the off-white portions of the feather. This general haze of color is often seen on real feathers. Also, while held at a distance from the sprayer, coat the rest of the feather with a fine mist that will render the feather off-white. The majority of real eagle feathers are not bright white like the bleached turkey feathers we're using for our projects. Many reproduction raptor feathers can be identified from across a large dance arena because of their blindingly white webbing.

Expensive air compressor tanks and high quality airbrushes aren't required. You can buy cans of compressed air and simple airbrush sprayers in the scale modeling sections of department and craft stores. When you're planning to paint just a couple dozen feathers for yourself this is a more economical way to go. Clean your equipment thoroughly after each use and it will serve you well through dozens of feathers.

Regardless of what airbrush system you chose, remember to wear a good quality air-filter mask when spraying and ventilate your work area. To help with applying the overspray, I have cut out one side of a cardboard box so as to lay the feather on the inside surface of the box while spraying. You need to have a backboard to support the feather or the airbrush will blow the feather around or separate the vanes and the paint will be applied unevenly.

Although I straighten every feather before I begin, I still finish out the feather with a final shaping and trimming, after the overspray has dried. I keep the temperature of the iron just below the steam setting, so as not to scorch the rachis or the vanes. I run the tip of the iron along the rachis to gently shape and mold each section of the rachis. (**Figure 2.8**) The sample feather is modeled after the second or third tail feather in, from the outer edge, so, it will need a curve in the rachis at the superior umbilicus. As the iron tip warms the rachis, I am able to mold the rachis in shape. I hold it there for a moment after I take the iron away and, as the rachis cools, it retains its new shape.

This step is really crucial in developing the illusion of a raptor feather. Consider real eagle feathers in three-dimensions and you'll see that they are not truly straight. There can be some side-to-side curve near the base of the feather quill depending on where the feather was located on the tail. Feathers from the outer edges have a pronounced curve and a very thin leading edge vane. (See reference photos & Tail Fan instructions in Chapter 5) All tail feathers have a front to back curve as part of their aerodynamic characteristics. **Figure 2.9** shows a feather in profile with the aerodynamic 'hump' at the superior umbilicus. Using the tip of the iron on the back side of the feather, I give it a slight front to back bend. (See also **Figure 5.81**) It may not be entirely necessary to go to such lengths, but, I believe that it is the small details that aide in the illusionary effect of an imitation raptor feather.

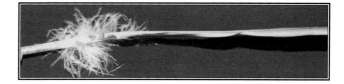

Figure 2.9   Shaping rachis with iron tip.

While you're shaping the rachis you can also use the iron to help preen the vane if it got messed up during the painting process. Hold the iron over the vane to warm it a bit. Run your fingers gently over the vane to preen the barbules back into shape. (**Figure 2.10**)

Figure 2.10
Preening the vane.

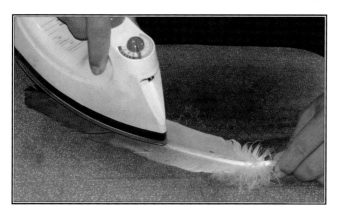

Figure 2.8   Shaping rachis with iron tip.

Trim your feathers with a sharp pair of barber's shears. Cut against the grain of the webbing as shown in **Figure 2.11**. Try to rest your arms on the table edge or chairs' arms to maintain a steady cut and avoid a ragged feather edge. A relatively simple tip to use when trimming is to print one of your reference photos of a real eagle feather at actual size. Cut out the feather and paste it onto heavy cardstock. Now, you have a template to use each time you trim and you know the curve will be accurate since you're following the ogive of a real feather.

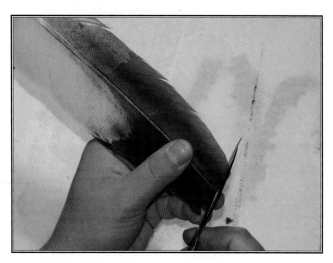

Figure 2.11 Trimming the ogive, against the grain with sharp shears.

One final touch that many feather painters overlook is the white line on the rachis. Scrape away some paint from the rachis to create a white line that extends up into the start of the dark section. Look closely on your reference photos and you'll see this detail is there.

At last, you're done. Congratulations… now go paint some more.

Figure 2.12
Finished immature Golden Eagle tail feather.

Figure 2.13 Close-up view of detail work.

Painting Hawk Feathers

The process for painting hawk feathers is a lot like what was described previously for eagle feathers. After sorting through pounds of feathers and selecting the proper size for hawk feathers, I straighten a bundle of same with the iron and scrape the rachis prior to painting. What follows are some photos and descriptions of the rest of the process that make these feathers uniquely hawk-like. Not all hawk wing feathers look alike, so be sure to review your reference photos. The following description is for a typical Red-tailed hawk secondary wing feather.

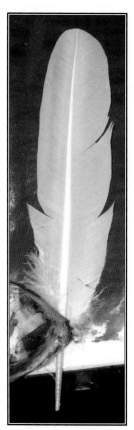

Figure 2.14 As I've done with this feather it can be helpful to do an initial trimming to roughly the size of the finished feather so you can better visualize where to paint the detail markings.

The bottom vanes are painted also for flurries. See the photo in **Figure 2.20,** Page 32.

Figure 2.15

I start each hawk feather by painting the upper-most bar on the tip. This end bar guides the placement of the rest of the markings on the feather.

Using a small to medium sized brush, paint the wide bars along the leading edge. There are generally five to seven bars on the leading edge.

Note that I paint the rachis
as I work my way down the feather.

Figure 2.16

Use a fine-tip brush to work in the thin lines. On hawk feathers, these thin lines of the trailing edge tend to match up with each wide bar on the leading edge. As you move toward the bottom of the feather, the lines get shorter, failing to reach the entire width of the vane.

I'm right handed and find it easiest to apply these lines by pulling the brush from left to right. On left-curve feathers I turn the feather around to get the trailing edge on the right, so I can pull the brush from left to right.

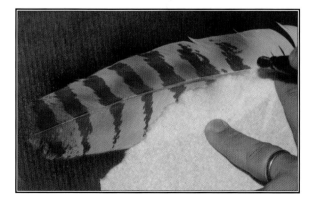

Figure 2.17

After you finish painting the main markings of the feather, set it aside to dry, while you work on a few others. The final touch on hawk wings is an overspray to color the background. In the photo at the left, I'm holding a paper towel in place while airbrushing the overspray color. The lower half of the trailing edge of hawk wings is generally white, so the paper towel helps guide the overspray. As with the eagle feather overspray, thin your paint with alcohol, to get a lighter color for airbrushing.

Figure 2.18
Overspray the background color on both the main feather and on the bottom sections that are stripped for flurries.

When the top-coat is dry, carefully strip the bottom sections of vane from the rachis and cut the rachis at the point where the lower vanes are still attached to the rachis.

Figure 2.19
Finished hawk feather.

Do a final shaping of the rachis with the tip of the iron, as described earlier in this chapter. Secondary wing feathers have a curve, as seen here, as well as front to back for aerodynamics.

I try to keep as much of the tip of the feather untrimmed as possible to give it a more natural look, but some trimming may be necessary.

The uses of secondary hawk wing feathers are practically endless, but there are also a multitude of uses for primary wing spikes. As such, I thought I should say a few words on creating hawk primaries. Primary wing spikes can be created by trimming turkey feathers to the proper shape or use an appropriately sized goose or chicken wing feather. Take the time to properly shape, and trim these so they look like raptor feathers.

The general appearance of Buteo hawks' wing spikes is a dark brown to black coloring over the entire length of the leading edge and halfway down the trailing edge vane. On some species, one can see some striations on the trailing edge, similar to those found on the secondary flight feathers. Review the photos in the reference section between chapters one and two.

Figure 2.20
This Crow bustle was made using the hawk flurries mentioned previously. These lower portions of the feathers that get stripped off also work well for Gustoweh, feather bonnet crown decoration and old-style bustles. See **Chapter 5** for instructions on these projects and how to create a modern Crow bustle like the one shown.

Painting Owl Feathers

Creating owl feathers is similar to hawk wings with a few principal differences. One important notation is the variation in pattern between feathers on the same wing. That is, not all secondary feathers on the same wing will look exactly alike. Study your reference photos carefully before you begin painting a feather. It may be helpful to decide which feather from a wing you're planning to replicate before you start painting.

Generally, the leading edge has five or six wide, horizontal bars with ragged edges. At the top end of the feather is a dark band across both vanes, positioned one centimeter from the end of the feather. Beginning one centimeter below this band, the leading edge has four or five wide bars perpendicular to the rachis. The trailing edge lines are not located exactly opposite the leading edge bars. While the first one, near the top of the feather, may be opposite the leading edge bar, the spacing between the subsequent lines increases such that the trailing edge lines are no longer positioned across from the leading edge bars. (See **Figure 2.21**)

Another important characteristic of owl feathers is the speckled pattern seen between the bars of the leading edge. Using a finely tipped brush, one can stipple in these markings between the bars. (See **Figure 2.22**) You can also achieve the same effect with a stout-bristled stencil brush. Use pieces of paper towel or scrap paper to guide the paint to the desired areas. The stippling of detail on an owl feather is quite time consuming, but, it should be noted, that attempts at time saving techniques often fail to produce a better product. The element of time is the only key factor necessary for producing a reasonable facsimile of a raptor feather.

Figure 2.22
Owl feather while hand-stippling detail marks with a fine-tipped brush.

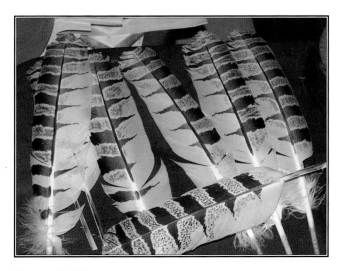

Figure 2.21
Sample of my painted owl feathers, prior to airbrushing the background color.

Once you have allowed your feathers to dry from painting the main markings, you can again use your airbrush to give the entire feather a characteristically owlish hue. The mixing of several dyes or paints may be necessary to produce the light brown-tan color of an owl feather. Refer to your reference photos once again for guidance. An important distinction is seen in the coloring of owl feathers. The entire feather should receive the overspray, with no white areas remaining on the bottom of the trailing edge, like hawk feathers. If you wash out the dye with alcohol for the overspray, it may be helpful to do the coloring before you do the detail stippling so the overspray doesn't cause your detail markings to run.

After the overspray coloring dries, complete the finishing shaping and trimming as you would with a hawk wing feather.

I find painting owl feathers one of the greatest challenges of feather painting and one the greatest joys as well. Contrary to what many people think, owl feathers were frequently employed among many of the indigenous nations across the country. There are a few tribes of the southern plains that do not use owl feathers, but, I feel owl feathers are generally underused in craftwork. Crow owl feather bonnets, dance bustles and the Blackfoot Dog Society bonnet in **Figure 2.23** below are just a couple examples of historical uses of owl feathers.

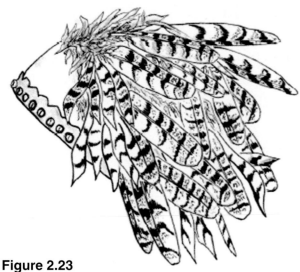

Figure 2.23
Blackfoot Dog Society bonnet of owl feathers.

Legal Imitations

As you may have discovered, the process of painting feathers is not a simple one. There are many benefits to creating your own raptor reproductions, but there is sometimes an easier way to go about it. Other than the obvious answer of paying someone else to paint your feathers, there is also the option of utilizing feathers that are natural mimics of raptor feathers. For example, there are a variety of chicken feathers with dark and light barring representing hawk and owl wings; Blue-eared Pheasant tail feathers look just like immature Golden Eagle tails; cinnamon turkey tail and wing feathers have a lovely rust color comparable to the Red-Tailed Hawk tail feather; Peahen wing and tail feathers can be excellent immature Bald Eagle feathers; and rooster coque has an iridescence that perfectly matches that of

magpie tails. These are just a few things to consider when searching for just the right feather additions to your dance outfit or craft project.

Figure 2.24
Natural turkey mimics. Upper left are Cinnamon Turkey tails. Feathers on the upper right are hybrid between Black Spanish and Royal Palm Heritage Breeds from www.portersturkeys.com. On the lower right is a composite of two hybrid turkey feathers to make an immature Bald Eagle plume.

Figure 2.25
Peafowl mimics. There are several breeds of peafowl and many of their feathers make great mimics. The upper right feathers look like sub-adult Bald Eagle, the bottom feathers are good owl mimics and the three feathers in the upper left are fine Ferruginous Hawk fakes.

Above Left: Brave Buffalo, Teton Sioux

In this studio portrait, Brave Buffalo is wearing a highly unusual headdress of mixed types of feathers, including what appear to be rather large owl tail feathers. He was an informant for Frances Densmore in her work on Teton Sioux music published in *Bureau of American Ethnology Bulletin 61, 1915*.

Above: Red Fish, Teton Sioux

This man is carrying an eagle wing fan and wearing a war bonnet of black and white eagle tail feathers, with smaller black and white eagle feathers used as side drops. Note the lack of a typical beaded or quilled browband on his bonnet. *Bureau of American Ethnology Bulletin 61, 1915.*

Left: Decorated War Honor Feathers

War honor feathers of the Chippewa war leader, Odjib'we. Each feather indicates he had taken a Sioux scalp and they are notched and decorated with rabbit skin and bits of ribbon on their tips. His prowess earned him the right to wear these eleven bald eagle feathers upright in a band around the head. *Bureau of American Ethnology Bulletin 53, Plate 5, 1915.*

High Hawk, Brule Sioux, 1907. Edward S. Curtis Photo. McKee-Reddick Collection.

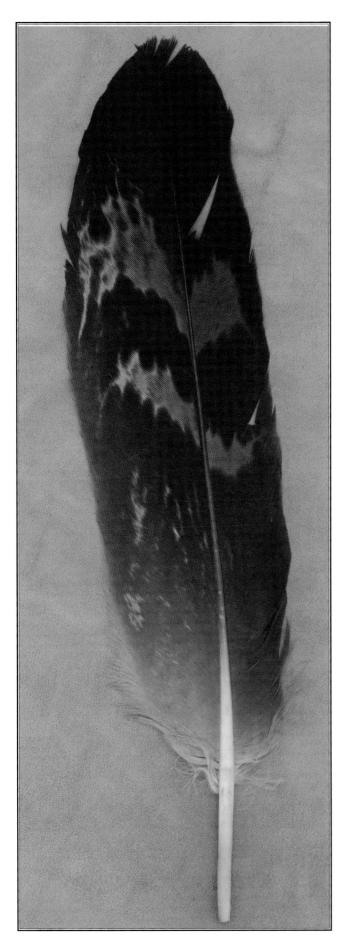

Chapter 3

Feather Alterations

$\mathcal{T}$ his chapter will present a variety of techniques that physically alter the structure of the feather. Many examples, both past and present, can be seen where the alteration of the feather creates an entirely new facet to the overall presentation of a craft project. It may help to consider that the use of feathers in a project is just as valuable a resource as the size and color of beads one may use. Throughout the nation you may see extraordinary works of art that utilize beads, quills and ribbons for decoration. And, it is readily apparent that such masterpieces were no doubt the product of tediously assembling the pieces with great planning and precision. One must approach the feather as an art medium in the same manner. Through various forms of manipulation, one can transform a simple thing of natural beauty, the feather, to a new level of artwork just as a sculptor creates from the natural beauty of stone a statue of striking character and presence.

Stripping

Separating the vane of the feather from the rachis has been a common technique since the times of antiquity when the bowyers added fletching to an arrow or perhaps an atlatl spear.

Begin near the top of the feather. Grasp one vane securely in your left hand while gently, but firmly, pulling the other vane away from the rachis with your right hand. Move your hand position down along the feather as you proceed to remove small segments at a time. If you are right-handed, it may be easier to strip with the right hand and use the left hand for holding the feather in position while you work. When done properly, one can remove the entire vane along the full length of the rachis without tearing the thin layer of membrane connecting the barbs together. After you have the first side done, turn the feather over and do the same to the other side.

These flurries of feather webbing can be used in a variety of projects, including old-style bustles, feathered bonnets, eastern style Gustoweh, or trim on a dance staff. The light webbing strips add three-dimensional bulk which brings a project more prominent attention and the fluttery effect imbues the article with life-like motion.

One often finds feathers that have had only the bottom two-thirds of the feather stripped, leaving a small portion of the feather tip intact.

If you parry the underside of the rachis below the remaining swatch of feather tip, the tip will have more fluttery motion as well. (See later section of this chapter on parrying.)

Figures 3.1 & 3.2 indicate several variations of the stripping and trimming methods found on historical projects. Of particular note of stripped feathers in historical pieces are the tail feather segments of the Raven Belts in the collection of the Peabody Museum, collected by Lewis & Clark. The rachis of the center tail is decorated with a quilled strip and the feathers to either side have had two inch segments of the vane stripped from the rachis. The remaining, bare rachis is painted red.

Serrated Edges & Cropping

The serrated effect is a simple one yet eye catching. To create the diamond-tip edges along a feather's perimeter, one does not need special shears, just a sharp pair of scissors.

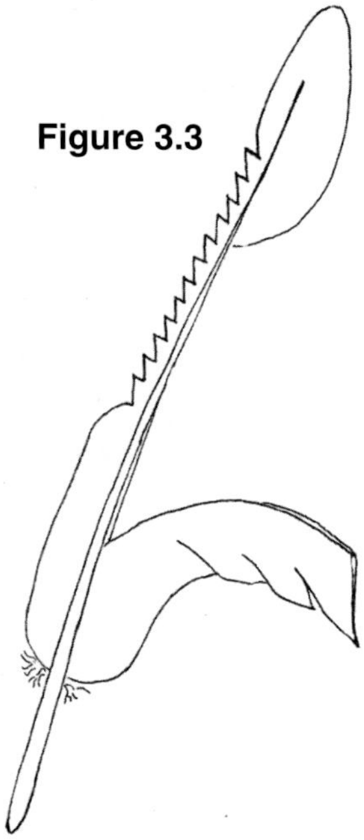

By making short cuts, ~1 cm long and ~1 cm apart, along the feather edge, perpendicular to the rachis, a portion of the webbing that is removed will leave a negative space that gives the appearance of a zig-zag line. This effect is the result of the grain of the feather barbs running at an angle from the rachis. By cutting at right angles to the rachis you are cutting across the lay of the barbs.

Figure 3.3

As you can see in **Figure 3.4** the serrated edge look is far simpler to produce than you may have originally expected.

While you have your scissors in hand, try this next technique that is actually as simple as it looks. Cropping feathers in half as seen in the sketch of **Figure 3.5** is a technique seen in a variety of historical pieces. Several of the museum examples of the Navajo war cap made from the head of a mountain lion have cropped raven feathers attached at the apex. Among the northern plains tribes the cropped feathers are also used on the crown of Strong Heart society, antelope horn, and split-horned bonnets. Other uses are on shields, rawhide rattles, hair ornaments and in feather wheels.

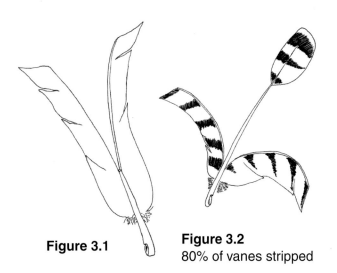

Figure 3.1

Figure 3.2
80% of vanes stripped

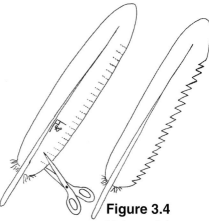

Figure 3.4

Make straight cuts perpendicular to the rachis to serrate the vane

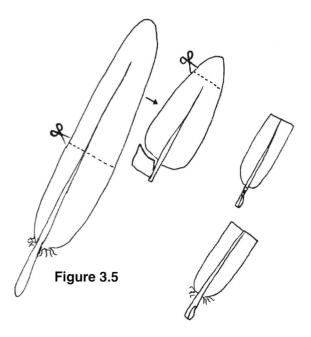

Figure 3.5

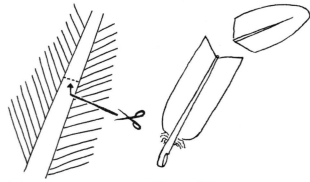

Figure 3.6   **Figure 3.7**

The resultant V-shape of the tip of the feather is very eye-catching in old-style bustles, arm bustles and feather wheels like those described in Chapter 5

Dyeing Feathers

You can find actual feather dyes to use in dye baths when desiring to dye the entire feather. These dyes are the same types used by the larger companies to create the brilliantly hued feathered costumes seen at Mardi Gras, and they work wonderfully. For an economical alternative, RIT clothing dye works very well and is easily purchased at most grocery or hardware stores.

Mix the dye liquid or crystals with enough water to cover the feathers you wish to dye. Vinegar can be added to the dye bath as a mordent to aide in setting the dye in the feathers. Long roasting pans work well for dye baths as the feathers can lay in the solution easily and enough water can be used to keep the feathers free flowing within the solution. The feathers can be added at any time as you bring the solution to a boil. Once boiling temperatures are reached, reduce heat to a slow simmer.

Since feathers are naturally water repellant and buoyant, it helps to use a wooden spoon, an expendable one, to keep the feathers submerged in the solution and the dye bath flowing freely over the feathers. The length of time needed for achieving the desired color may vary so it is best to stay close and stir regularly. To check your feathers, carefully remove one and rinse in cold water. Once the excess dye is rinsed away you will have a better idea of the finished color of the feather. As a general rule, keep the feathers in the pan until they are a shade darker than the desired hue before removing and rinsing.

Figures 3.5 indicates how one could get two cut feathers from a single feather by using the upper half of the feather being cropped. From this piece, strip the vane from the bottom one inch of rachis and crop the very tip straight across. Add loops or self-loop the bases of each piece and you now have two feathers to add to your project.

As the sketch to the left shows, making a simple, transverse cut perpendicular to the rachis will suffice. For a slightly more unique look, cut only the rachis and not the vane (see **Figure 3.6**).

Use just the tip of a sharp scissors to do this. When you remove the cropped piece, the natural grain of the vane will have a V-shape, as sketched in **Figure 3.7**, instead of the straight line cut.

Lay the feathers out on paper towels to dry. A more aggressive method of drying feathers is to create a drying box. Place the wet feathers into a small to medium sized cardboard box. Cut a hole in one side of the box and insert the barrel of a hair dryer. Turn the hair dryer on low speed, low temperature to begin drying the feathers. The box keeps the feathers from flying all over the house while drying. Kick the blower speed up to high so the feathers blow around inside the box. This will help restore the marabou of feathers after their bath.

I suggest the dyeing process be completed outside as opposed to using your best pot and slotted spoon in the kitchen as the dye bath may splatter while simmering and leave spots of color around your kitchen stove. A camp stove or side burner of a grill works well when heating dye baths.

Dyed feathers can be used for many projects. A plethora of museum collections contain old-style bustles and bonnets containing yellow, orange, red, green and purple feathers. Red eagle fluffs were employed on tips of bustle or bonnet feathers. Several bonnets have entire eagle and hawk tail and wing feathers dyed red. Several old-style, crow-belt, bustles exhibit feathers that are dyed on the bottom half only.

Among those crafters involved in making historic reproductions, dyeing pheasant tail feathers black as a replica of magpie and raven tails has proven most effective for the production of Dog Soldier headdresses like the one worn by Mato Topa in Karl Bodmer's sketches. Such a bonnet was used in the movie Last of the Dogmen, created by Bill & Kathy Brewer of Indian Images.

Trimming Feathers

As I've said before, we must view feathers as an art medium. By sculpting and shaping the feather we create a new visual appeal or enhance the illusion of a raptor feather mimic. When trimming feathers it is important to use a very sharp scissor, preferably barber's shears. Make your cuts against the grain of the vane so as to avoid pressing the vane in towards the rachis and resulting in a ragged edge. More detailed instructions for trimming the ogive of painted feathers can be found in chapter two. Here are a few variations on the methods of trimming feathers.

It may seem an obvious suggestion, but the use of a template can be a great aide in making consistent cuts on feathers. Draw your patterns on heavy poster board or thin plastic. Laying your pattern over your feather you can make consistently smooth, accurate ogives. The use of a rotary cutter can also make quick work of the trimming process if one trims the feathers while they're laying flat on a cutting surface. If one has access to real feathers, use a pencil to trace your patterns and you'll be sure to have the right ogive every time. One can also take digital images of real feathers, enlarge the feather to actual size and print a copy. With this as your guide you would once again achieve the perfect curve.

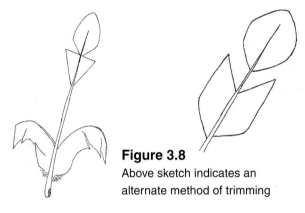

Figure 3.8
Above sketch indicates an alternate method of trimming

Splicing Feathers

Splicing, as the name implies, is the act of combining two different feathers. There exist several reasons and applications of splicing but a popular result of splicing is the creation of an extra-long and wide feather that more closely resembles the size of a real eagle feather.

Carefully remove the trailing edge vane from one feather and the leading edge vane from the other feather. By welding the trailing edge vane you just stripped off in place of the leading edge vane you just removed, you can produce a long, wide feather that more closely matches the dimensions of a real eagle feather. Before attaching the stripped trailing vane to the rachis, gather all materials and have them close at hand. Masking tape and sewing pins are useful in holding the vane in place while the glue dries. Also, straighten the rachis of the feather that will be the base feather onto which you will be applying the new vane. It is much easier to apply the new vane to a straightened rachis instead of a curved one and the glues used in splicing may not withstand the heat involved in straightening process

Fletching glue sold in archery supply stores is specifically designed for gluing feathers so it is a good choice. Glue that is more viscous is advantageous in that it stays in place on the rachis instead of running onto the vane. A quick drying epoxy can also be used successfully but be sure to select an adhesive that will not discolor when dry or after aging.

With the fine tip of the applicator bottle apply an amount of glue to the rachis. Near the tip of the feather the rachis isn't thick enough to permit pins to hold the vane in place so masking tape can work well on the first several inches. Apply glue to just a few inches of the rachis at a time as you work along to glue down the new vane and hold in place with pins. It may also be helpful to apply the glue to a larger section of the rachis and allow it to begin to dry to the point of becoming tacky. At this point, when the vane is applied it will adhere almost instantly and thus stay in place better without the use of pins or tape.

After allowing sufficient time to dry, you can remove the pins and tape then proceed to painting your newly created feathers.

Once the splicing technique has been mastered, there are several other applications to creating unique feathers. By using large goose primaries, the spliced feathers will not need coloring to create a realistic raptor mimic. The splicing of Canada goose wing spikes produces a large, dark feather that closely resembles the secondary wing feathers of an eagle.

Figure 3.9
Spliced goose feathers with imitation eagle fluff attached at base. These feathers came from a domestic goose, not the wild Canada Goose, hence the spotting and detail marks. Even under close scrutiny it's hard to see the splice seam.

Another project that may be worth your efforts is the production of an extra large spike feather to more appropriately match the dimensions of an eagle wing spike. The turkey wing spikes one can purchase for bustle or wing fan making are neither long nor wide enough to simulate eagle wing spikes. An eagle wing has a wider section near the base of the feather on both the leading and trailing edge. This feather design is known as emarginate primaries. (**Figure 3.10**) By splicing in a section of vane from a turkey secondary wing feather along the base of a primary one can build a whole new wing spike.

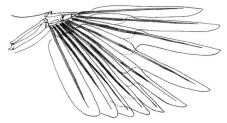

Figure 3.10
Emarginate primaries. The dotted lines indicate how a portion of the trailing edge widens. I've also include the attachment points of the feathers to the bones.

Begin with selecting a prime turkey wing spike and proceed to straighten it. Choose a wide secondary wing feather and strip the trailing vane from the rachis. Before attaching this vane it may be necessary to extend the rachis of the wing spike. There are several ways to do this.

One method, known as imping, is to crop the spikes' rachis where the vane stops, superior umbilicus, and add to it the bottom half of a rachis from another spike feather. Heavy wire inserted into the rachis of the extension (**Figure 3.11**) will slide up into the rachis of the spike and act as a splint to hold them more securely. Use a small dab of adhesive on the cut to hold them together. Once this splice is completed and the glue dry trim the newly attached section of secondary wing feather to the appropriate shape of an emarginated primary.

Figure 3.11

Another method is to attach the secondary vane to the bottom of the spike feather in such a fashion that the new addition continues all the way to the tip of the calamus (inferior umbilicus). At this point the vaned sections will match the length of vaned sections of an eagle wing.

By adding a dowel rod insert to the spike feather you will gain another four to five inches in length of the overall feather to match the overall length of an eagle feather. (*See next section for tips on extending feathers*) This extension would most likely be disguised under whatever you employ in decorating the base of the feather in the construction of the bustle or fan set.

An alternative method of splicing two feathers together is to bisect the rachis along the length of the shaft. A scalpel-sharp blade is necessary for a smooth incision. This technique is easier along the lower portions of the rachis but becomes considerably more difficult near the feather tip as the rachis thins. Two cuts are necessary. One begins at the aftershaft and extends the length of the feather while the second is a small cross-cut to remove the split section from the rest of the shaft. Extensive practice is recommended before attempting this technique on your best feathers. In order to use this technique for larger eagle tail feathers, one should bisect the rachis of two different feathers, one right one left. As before, you must remove the leading edge of one feather and the trailing edge of the other. Insert the trailing edge section into the slot created by removing the leading edge and glue in place with a durable epoxy. Pins and tape can be used to hold the new addition in place while the adhesive dries. This style of splice may be more applicable when splicing in a wider section at the base of a wing spike to create a more proportionately sized wing spike.

One drawback to the cut and splice method as opposed to the strip and splice is that the seam is more visible, but you can employ a decorative technique to disguise the splice seam.

Another interesting application of yet another splicing technique is in the creation of faux magpie tail feathers. Magpie tail and wing feathers were frequently used by native peoples of a variety of prairie and plains tribes. Magpies may not be classified as raptors by the scientific community, but they are designated as a protected species by the USFWS. As such, the possession, sale or barter of their feathers is restricted in the United States. Magpie wing feathers can be reproduced by painting but the iridescence of the tail feather makes painting imitations a challenge at best.

The readily available rooster coque feathers are an excellent mimic in color and size, but there is one major drawback. These rooster feathers lack a sufficiently stiff rachis, tending to bend and curl easily which isn't quite the nature of a magpie tail feather. Carefully strip the vanes from the tail of a pheasant feather. Glue a rooster coque feather along the top of the bare shaft of the pheasant rachis. With this simple method you can produce a quality magpie tail mimic that not only has the dark colored vane with dazzling, green-purple iridescence with the strength and durability necessary for use in a variety of projects.

Feather Extensions

Occasionally one may find it necessary to increase the length of the feathers by adding an extension to the calamus. The fundamental principle is to insert an extension rod into the hollow shaft of the calamus and secure it in place. Several techniques and materials can accomplish this and your selections may be determined by the intended use of the feather. What follow are several techniques I've used successfully in a variety of craft projects over the years.

When extending turkey feathers for bustle and fan work, wooden dowel rods of 1/8" to 3/16" work well. Many different materials can be utilized as extension rods so feel free to make your choice based on availability to you. Other options include carbon or aluminum arrow shaft pieces, kabob skewers, bamboo chopsticks, etc. Arrow shaft scraps can often be procured for free from your local archery store. Chopsticks may come free with a good Chinese take-out but most grocery stores offer chopsticks or bamboo skewers for a reasonable price.

The diameter of the extension rod should be such that it fills the inner hollow of the shaft. Begin by cutting off the tip of the calamus to access the hollow shaft and fill the inner shaft of the quill with glue. Some brands of epoxy dispensers have an applicator tip which facilitates filling the hollow shaft with epoxy before inserting the extensor rod. While epoxy is a more secure adhesive, the use of water soluble glues can be advantageous. Years from now when you wish to re-use those bustle feathers for another project or when repairs become necessary, you can soak the feather in warm water to remove an extension rod and clean up the feather quill in minutes.

Insert the extension rod as far as you can within the hollow quill and hold in place for a few minutes while the glue begins to set. If you can, lay the feather down at an angle so that the glue does not run back out of the feather along the extension rod but remains within the feather while it dries completely.

After the glue has set properly you can cut the extension rods of each feather to the necessary length to keep them even. Line up the feathers with the tips even across a line before marking a line along the extension to be cut. Apply a loop at the base of the extension rod to allow for stringing all the feathers together in order. (See also Chapter 5, Northern Plains Style Bonnet, for another method of feather extensions specifically recommended for use on bonnets.)

The series of four sketches in **Figures 3.12-3.15**, below, illustrate these simple steps for extending feathers.

You may end up drilling a hole through the feather quill and dowel rod for a guide line when stringing these feathers together for a bustle or fan set so that too would act as extra insurance for holding the extension rods in place (See Chapter 5 on bustle construction.)

An alternative material for feather extensions is a feather quill from a scrap feather. Strip the vanes from a feather and cut the rachis just above the superior umbilicus. Insert this section into the hollow calamus of your feather and glue in place. The extension section may need to be shaved down to fit inside the hollow feather shaft. This method becomes particularly useful in bonnet construction (See Chapter 5 for more details). Shrink-wrap tubing can help with such a splice. Cut the main feather off and insert the tip halfway into a two inch section of the tubing. Into the other end insert the scrap quill extension. A little heat will shrink the tubing tightly over the spliced area and the tubing will be covered with any base decorations. Details of this technique are given in Chapter 5 on wing fans. (Thanks go out to Craig Jones for sharing another great tip.)

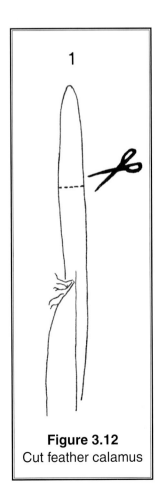

Figure 3.12
Cut feather calamus

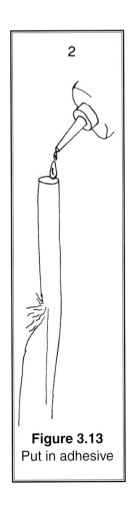

Figure 3.13
Put in adhesive

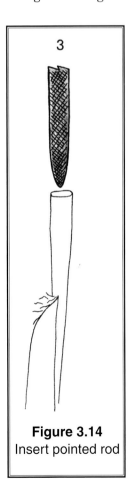

Figure 3.14
Insert pointed rod

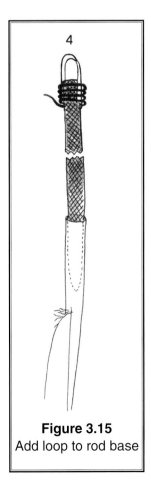

Figure 3.15
Add loop to rod base

Self-Loop & Added Loops

The majority of projects that incorporate feathers require the existence of a loop at the calamus to facilitate stringing several feathers together. One such example is shown in **Figure 3.16**. What follows here are several of a large variety of methods for adding the necessary loop to a feather.

Figure 3.16

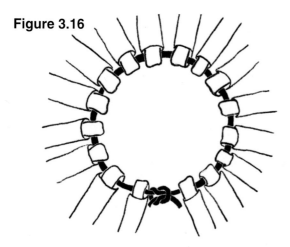

Many original artifacts that employ feathers utilize a self-splice loop. The process is a simple one as illustrated in **Figure 3.17**. Begin by making a shallow cut on the ventral side of the calamus, like scooping out a half-moon shape. Once you have excised the piece of quill, bend the tip of the quill over and insert the tip into the hollow of the calamus. Use glue to hold in place or wrap with sinew. The use of real sinew works best as it is not only more apropos for a reproduction piece but also holds fast once the moistened sinew dries hard. The cutting and bending can be facilitated by soaking the quill in warm water for a few minutes. The softened quill is less likely to split while being cut and bent back upon itself.

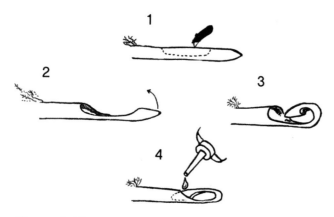

Figure 3.17
These sketches show the process of creating a self-loop on a feather.

The self loop is simple enough to perform but there comes a time when a little more ingenuity is necessary. Some of the painted hawk and owl feathers available for purchase or one you finish yourself will lack a hollow calamus because of shortening the larger turkey feather to the appropriate size of a hawk or owl feather. The lack of a hollow calamus to insert the tip of the quill may seem like an insurmountable challenge but there is actually a simple solution. **Figures 3.18 & 3.19** below illustrate these simple steps.

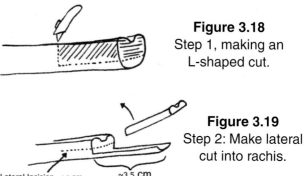

Figure 3.18
Step 1, making an L-shaped cut.

Figure 3.19
Step 2: Make lateral cut into rachis.

Begin with an L-shaped cut on the ventral portion of the rachis to remove a section of the rachis tip. The long leg of the L-cut should be approximately 3.5-4 centimeters. You can scrape excess pith from the rachis but leave the dorsal part of the rachis as illustrated in **Figure 3.19**. Step 2 is a lateral incision along the length of the rachis but do not remove another portion of the rachis.

In the last step, fold over the extension of the rachis and insert it into the lateral slit (See **Figure 3.20**). Glue the inserted section into place or secure with real sinew.

Figure 3.20
Step 3, insert the strip of rachis into the lateral cut and glue in place.

While self-loops are often the best bet for reproduction pieces, they aren't always desirable for contemporary work. There are many alternatives to choose from, but I have chosen two specific techniques to present herein.

Loop Additions

The addition of a leather/rawhide loop at the calamus tip is a simple procedure. With a little practice with the whipping technique illustrated here, one can apply leather loops to large number of feathers in a short time frame.

Begin by folding the sinew to form a loop. Lay this loop along the top of the feather and on the leather loop. While holding all the pieces in place with the thumb and forefinger of one hand, use the other to tightly wrap the sinew around the feather quill, securing the leather and the original sinew loop on the calamus. Pass the tail of the sinew thread up through the sinew loop. Finish by pulling the original tail of the sinew loop to close the loop and secure with it the tail of the wrapped sinew thread. By pulling the loop under the wraps you just made with the sinew the tails are held tightly in place by the wraps themselves so no knots or glue are necessary. Snip each sinew thread tail and move on to the next feather.

Figure 3.21

Wrap thread around calamus
to secure leather & thread loop

A wonderful alternative to the leather loop was conveyed to me by friend and fellow traditional dancer Craig Jones. He uses the plastic binding strap on boxes of copy paper and tears them into long strips. These strips are cut into segments of 3-5 centimeters, folded in half and glued into the hollow cavity of the calamus (See Figure 3.24). These plastic loops can be used on feathers or the hollow shaft of a carbon arrow extension rod inserted in the hollow calamus. (See previous section of this chapter on feather extension methods and materials.)

Other plastic or stiff rawhide materials would also work well for this looping technique. Plastic zip-strips would be excellent and inexpensive alternative.

Figure 3.22

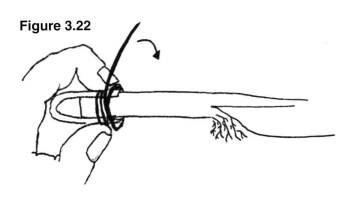

Other plastic or stiff rawhide materials would also work well for this looping technique. Plastic zip-strips would be excellent and inexpensive alternative.

Figure 3.23

Pull

An ancillary benefit to this technique is the absence of a bump or ridge formed by wrapping the loop on the outer sheath of the calamus. When decorating the base of the feather for a bustle or fan, the smooth surface of the outer calamus provides a better surface with which to work. Furthermore, the stiff loop, as opposed to a flexible piece of leather, will aide in keeping the feathers in order instead of bunching up, one on top of the other like mis-stacked ranks of wood.

Figure 3.24

NocBay Trading Company has an interesting looping technique presented on their website that also utilizes some modern materials. After snipping off the clasp end of a safety pin with wire cutters the remaining wires are attached to the base of the calamus with glue and sinew wrappings. This leaves a small wire loop at the base of the feather for stringing feathers together. The wire posts can be alternately secured by bending them at right angles to have them inserted through holes in the calamus. Poke holes in the calamus with a sharp awl. The wires will snap into place when inserted into the hollow quill. Use pliers to bend the wire stubs flat against the feather calamus thus locking the wire loop in place.

The sketches below are alternative methods of feather attachments for stringing feathers together or for adding single feathers to a part of a dancer's outfit. Nearly all of these are methods recorded in use on historic artifacts.

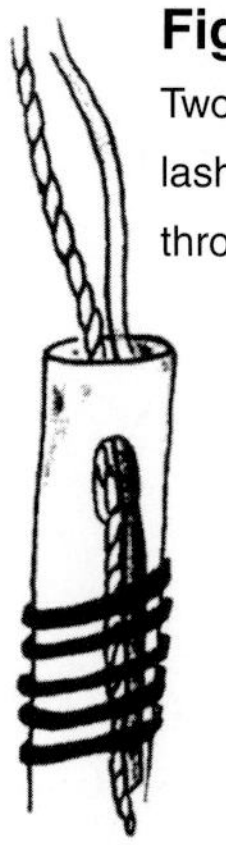

Figure 3.25
Two individual threads lashed in place & passed through hole in quill.

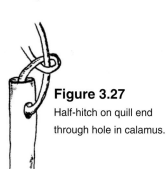

Figure 3.26
Single thread acting as bridle. Taped to keep quill from splitting.

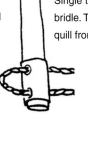

Figure 3.27
Half-hitch on quill end through hole in calamus.

Figure 3.28
Simple overhand knot in string to keep feather in place.

Figure 3.29
Self-loop & lashed leather thong.

Figure 3.30
Leather thong lashed on with sinew.

Figure 3.31
Short bend around quill through hole in quill.

Figure 3.32
Quill is split, leather thong inserted & wrapped with sinew.

Figure 3.33
Larks head loop around quill. My adaptation of historic example

Parrying Feathers

Parrying feathers is the process of thinning the ventral rachis. The flexible rachis will allow the feather to shutter and flash in the slightest breeze and imbue your article with life-like animation, just as the golden Aspen comes to life with autumnal breath. Parried feathers work well on old-style bustles and are also found on a variety of headdresses such as the Strong Heart Society and antelope horn bonnets in the collection of the Beuchel Museum in St. Francis, SD. Parried feathers are also nice for lightweight axillary feathers worn in the hair. A variety of museum specimens of men's wapegnaka (hair ornaments) have parried feathers as well.

Figure 3.34

After some experimentation with a variety of techniques I found that the best method is to make use of a Dremel tool. This little electric wonder has different types of sanding bits that work very well for thinning the rachis of a feather. A standard drum sander (see **Figure 3.34**) works well for most projects but a conical shaped sander may be useful at times. Using just the tip of a conical sander allows you to sand feathers with a thin rachis with less of a chance for damaging the vane. Remember, practice safety, wear a quality dust mask and protective eyewear when sanding feathers.

46

One can shave the rachis down so far as to leave just a 3/16 inch (3-4mm) strip of the dorsal side of the rachis and it will still remain securely intact. The keratin protein fibers that form feathers are quite strong. (See **photos 3.11 & 3.12**) Practice on some scrap feathers prior to attempting to parry your best feathers.

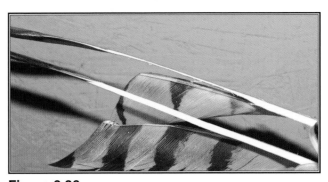

Figure 3.36
The photo to the left shows a comparison of one feather parried (top) next to one that hasn't been parried.

Figure 3.35
This side view of a parried hawk feather shows how the flexible rachis allows the tip to flutter & sway.

Taping the Underside of Feathers

Keeping feathers looking new can be a time consuming process. During an average weekend of pow-wowing feathers get ruffled, split, bent, and torn. Steaming and ironing to preen the feathers back into shape can be a lot of work.

Among his many idioms of wisdom, Benjamin Franklin reminds us that prevention is better than a cure. By taping the underside of feathers in your feather clusters, you can prevent a lot of the headaches and hassle of having to fix your feathers regularly.

Clear packing tape will work best. Carefully layer the clear tape until all sections of vane are covered on either side of the rachis. Use a sharp scissor to trim any excess tape around the perimeter of the feather. The shiny, reflective surface of the tape can be marred by sanding lightly with 200 grit sandpaper.

Parade Time
This mounted Kiowa warrior is wearing a large eagle feather warbonnet with trailer and is carrying a loose fan and lance, also of eagle tail feathers. Even his horse has a feather tied into its tail. *McKee-Reddick Collection Photo.*

47

Washakie, Chief of the Eastern Shoshone, ca. 1881. *McKee-Reddick Photo Collection.*

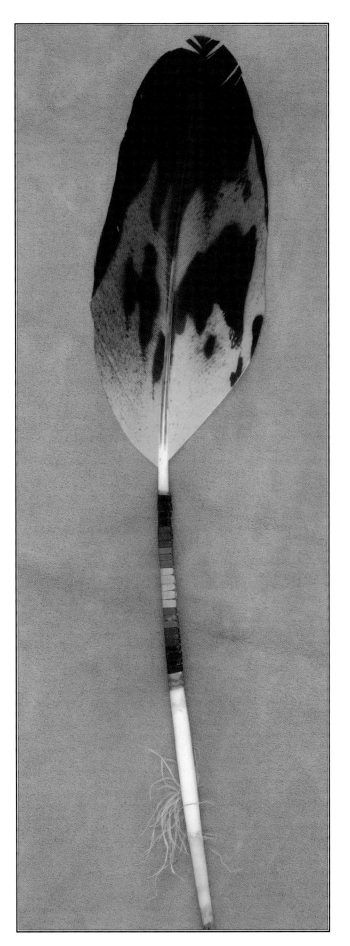

Chapter 4

Feather Adornments

As a great admirer of the Lord's aviary creations, I find it hard to improve upon the natural beauty of the feather. It doesn't really matter what species of bird donated the feather. Whether it possesses a shimmering iridescence or a dun hue, the slender curving rachis of a secondary wing feather or the flexible shaft of an undertail plume that dances on the wind, it is the greatest challenge to find a flaw in their beauty and design. And yet, while the Lord imbued them with beauty He didn't necessarily color coordinate them to our dance outfits. Fortunately there are a variety of simple methods for dressing up your feathers to match your dance clothes.

Decorating the Feather Base

Generally speaking, the calamus is decorated with a covering of some kind after adding a loop for stringing several feathers together or for attaching in the hair. The materials used for decoration will vary based on the intended use of the feathers. A variety of feathers employ a red wool wrapping, also known as a 'firecracker'. This is most commonly seen on bonnet feathers, both new and old. The material you choose to cover the quill, whether wool, leather or other, is simply wrapped around the base and held in place by either sewing the seam, an adhesive, or wrapping another cord around the covering. Sewing the seam certainly takes more time but one can get a very neat, snug look to the material as the stitches pull the material around the feather. Sewing the seams is my preferred method of attachment when preparing bustle and staff feathers. The running stitch and whip stitch (**Figures 4.1 & 4.2** respectively) are quick and easy as well as often seen on museum artifacts. The baseball stitch was rarely used.

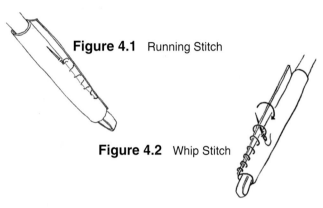

Figure 4.1 Running Stitch

Figure 4.2 Whip Stitch

When the material is covering a short section of feather as opposed to an extension rod in addition to the feather a thread wrap at the top and bottom of the material covering is sufficient to hold it in place. When researching the preparation of bonnet feathers or bustle trailer feathers one finds the red wool held in place by wrapping the wool in several ways.

Three suggestions are illustrated in **Figure 4.3**; wraps at the top and bottom; wrapping at top, middle and bottom; and spiral wrap from top to bottom. The thread used can be anything from sinew (both real and imitation), rawhide lace, leather, cotton twine, linen cord, or pericardium. Regardless of the material chosen for the thread, it is generally white to contrast with the red wool as an aesthetic visual affect.

Figure 4.3

Naturally, we cannot discount the effectiveness and time-saving benefit of simply gluing the material covering into place. Water soluble glues are your best bet. Test the glue on some scrap materials to verify the glue will sufficiently bind the wool or leather to the feather without discoloration or distortion of the fibers. Glue cover material in place and wrap with strips of 1"x12" cotton cloth to hold in place while the glue dries. This works much like wrapping a wet roach onto a stick to form and shape it while it dries.

For a more modern flare, many craftsman employ colored electrical tape to dress up the base of feathers or a feathers' extension. With a little planning one can create eye catching geometric patterns with different colors of tape on the feather extension rods of a bustle. Several of the major craft supply companies offer colored electrical tape. One cautionary note when applying plastic electrical tape, do not pull the tape and stretch it too much while winding it around a feather or extension rod. The tape may eventually pull itself loose as the tape relaxes to its original shape, much like a stretched rubber band snapping back to its original form.

Another method of dressing up feathers very much in vogue today is thread wrapping. The use of colorful threads like embroidery floss can open a full palette of possibilities for decorating feathers. A unique tool that becomes indispensable when thread wrapping comes from the flytiers toolbox, a bobbin holder (see **Figure 4.6**). The bobbin holder keeps tension on the thread while wrapping and the guide post where the thread comes off the spool allows for layering your thread with greater precision along the feather quill, rachis, feather extension rod, or rawhide slat for mimicking quillwork. Fly tying shops also carry a wide range of threads used in fly tying. One can find thin ribbon-like threads, thick fuzzy thread and all in brilliant colors to draw attention to you feathers.

The use of thread wrapping creates some opportunities for artistic design that go beyond the employment of colors in a flat medium by allowing for three-dimensional structures created along with the infusion of color. By building up a mound of thread, one can create three-dimensional patterns within the colors of the thread. Some crafters slide a bead onto the quill and glue it into place where they plan for a mound of thread. This saves some time and thread as you cover the bead with thread.

A predecessor to thread wrapping may be the use of yarn and/or macramé cord. A Northern Cheyenne bonnet [NA.205.9] in the collection of the Plains Indian Museum of the Buffalo Bill Historical Center (BBHC) utilizes blue yarn wrappings on the base of each feather. One note of caution when using yarn is to wrap the yarn in the correct direction around the object. Wrapping in a given direction will result in the twisted strands of yarn becoming unwound while the opposite direction will keep the yarn threads tightly twisted together when wrapping.

Figure 4.4

This feather illustrates the use of thread-wrapping, feather cropping, and feather layering at the base and center unite to create a singular work of art. Rhinestone spots & hair tufts on the tip can also be used.

Regardless of which material one chooses to decorate the calamus, the addition of small feather fluffs or colorful contour feathers can be an excellent compliment to the artistry of the larger feather. Florette feathers in a variety of colors are offered by a number of craft suppliers. Figure 4.3 illustrates several examples of feather additions under the base wrapping. Such feathers can be laid in place on top of the rachis and held in place with a few wraps of thread or sinew or a quick-drying adhesive. The wool, electrical tape, thread, etc. will then cover this area. The artistry of layering small, colorful contour feathers at the base of larger feathers for scalp feathers or fan sets is limited only by ones creativity.

Figure 4.5 shows an example of elaborate feather layering at the base of a feather. The front feather has had clear packing tape applied on the underside so that sections of the feather could be carefully cut out with a sharp knife. This allows the color of the feather underneath to show through in a decorative pattern. Another useful tool taken from a fly-tiers' toolbox is the spring-tweezers (see Figure 4.6). These remain closed until squeezed and their small jaw grasps feathers delicately but securely while setting them in place for such precise work depicted in Figures 4.4 & 4.5.

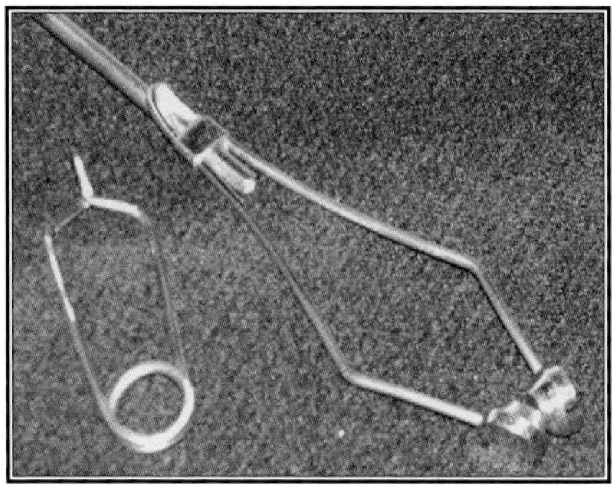

Figure 4.6

Figure 4.5

Perhaps the most common method of 'dressing up' a feather is the application of paint, fur or leather spots. The designs could be made from thin leather, white being the more common choice; paints in a variety of colors to compliment your outfit; or colored electrical tape cut into shapes. For a real dazzling flash, use reflective tape or small rhinestones that glisten and reflect brilliant flashes of light.

When gluing fur or leather spots on the feather choose a water soluble adhesive. In the future you can remove the leather spots and wash the feather clean of glue residue to recycle the feather for another project.

Paints for clothing can be purchased at may craft supply stores. These come in bottles with a pointed applicator tip to make fine lines or small dots. These are fantastic for making simple but eye-catching designs along the rachis of a feather to imitate quillwork or simply place spots along a feather vane.

A unique method of vane decoration found on feathers of old-style bustles of the late 19th and early 20th centuries is the application of printed text with the use of rubber stamps. Mercantile companies who offered feathers for purchase would ad-

vertise their store or the name of a product on feathers they sold. One can have a rubber stamp made at the local Staples or Office Depot and begin stamping feathers. Either research historic articles for names of mercantile stores and trading posts from the west or create your own fictitious name.

Figure 4.7

A method less often seen today but found among museum artifacts is the addition of colored fluffs through the rachis. Carefully cut a longitudinal slit in the rachis through which to pass small downy feathers (see **Figure 4.7**). This can be done on the dorsal or ventral rachis. Thin ribbon can also be used instead of feather fluffs. Roach feathers as early as pre-1850 exist in museum collections with ribbon decorations through the rachis. [Peabody Museum #99-12-10/53057]

Figure 4.8 illustrates a rather advanced method, also a historically documented method, of feather alteration and adornment. After stripping away the vane from several inches of the rachis along the center of the shaft, use a sharp knife to carefully split the rachis lengthwise. Some removal of the inner pith as in parrying will make the two stems flexible. Add fluffs, plumes, horsehair or ribbon to the tips of the two stems in any variety of colors and styles. This technique transitions us into the next main topic of feather adornments.

Figure 4.8

Feather Tip Decoration

As **Figure 4.8** clearly shows, one can easily add feather fluffs and plumes to the tip of a feather. A few wraps of sinew or cotton thread would generally be all one needs to hold the feathers in place. If using anything other than real sinew, a light layer of glue to hold the wraps tight is recommended.

There is more to dressing up the tips of feathers than the addition of more feathers. Horse hair or strands of cow tail hair were often used. Cow tail hair has the unique property of being curly instead of straight like horsehair. If all you have to work with is horse hair you can curl that to get the same effect. A curling iron certainly works but another simple method is to braid the hair tightly while it is wet. Once it dries undo the braid and the hair will retain the curves and kinks from the braid.

A common decoration is to have hair or ribbon extensions off the tip of the feather held in place by glue instead of sinew wrappings. In these cases one usually employs something else to cover up the ends of the hair or ribbon being glued in place. A leather dot is a simple enough method or perhaps a piece of white ermine fur to add a three-dimensional aspect to the decoration. Another very old and popular material is Gypsum. Gypsum is a naturally occurring mineral (Calcium sulfate) found in a crystalline structure and varying in color from white to grey or pinkish-red. When pulverized and mixed with an adhesive the crystalline structure of Gypsum can be dabbed onto the end of the feather where it will dry into a glistening drop. If pure Gypsum isn't readily available one can use drywall joint compound powder or Plaster of Paris powder in the same way. Both of these materials have Gypsum as a main ingredient so you generally get a nice effect.

Quillwork

There are a variety of methods of quillwork that can be, and historically have been, employed in the decoration of feathers. Perhaps the most commonly recognized method is the attachment of a quill-wrapped strip along a feather's rachis. These strips are generally held in place with sinew wrappings at the base of the feather near the superior umbilicus and again at the tip.

Figure 4.9 shows a method of trimming the base material to a slender extension for wrapping at the tip of a feather. Also as indicated one can easily include some feathers or horsehair additions in the tip wrappings. Many good books and internet resources provide detailed instructions on the technique of quill-wrapping. Find one that provides plenty of illustrations and photos that clearly show each step of the process and practice, practice, practice to become proficient. In that time of practice you will soon have a bundle of strips ready to decorate feathers.

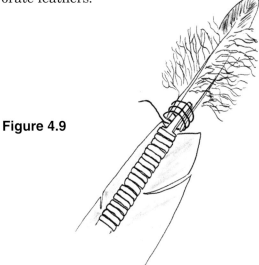

Figure 4.9

Rawhide is generally considered the traditional material of choice for quill-wrapped strips but many other materials can be substituted for rawhide. Some historical pieces show the use of thin wooden slats. [Raven belt, Peabody Museum #99-12-10/53057] Wooden stir-sticks are a fine, modern source for quill wrapping. Another modern material is plastic zip-strips, also known as zip ties. Snip the buckle, boxed, end off and you have a thin, rigid material for wrapping quills around.

Before we get too far from our focus on feathers let's consider what materials are used in quill-wrapping. Porcupine quills are certainly the most common material but bird quills (rachis) were also employed in the same techniques of porcupine quillwork. Prepare the rachis for quill-wrapping by stripping the vanes from the rachis. Shave the rachis down just as you would for parrying. The dorsal strip of rachis that remains is softened for flexibility and wrapped just as one would porcupine quills. These can also be dyed in the same manner as one would porcupine quills. Bird quills have been used in several quill-embroidery techniques by indigenous peoples from much of North America.

Plant matter like corn husk strips or long, thin, grass-like leaves were also used historically and can be used today as well. Raffia found in craft stores is a good substitute for porcupine quills. Plant matter and raffia can also be dyed prior to wrapping. Thread-wrapped strips can also be quickly done with the aide of the fly-tier's bobbin holder. The plethora of radiant hues available in threads makes the possibilities nearly endless for dressing up feathers with colorful thread-wrapped strips.

The photo to the left presents a lesser known example of quill-wrapped feather. This technique of quillwork is a bit more advanced but is an ancient technique use for decorating thin, round objects.

Begin by stripping the vanes from a section of the feather that is to be quilled. Secure the waxed thread at each end of the stripped section to be quilled with a length of that cord running between each end, pulled taught. A second thread, we'll call it the fastening line, is attached to that taught strand running parallel to the feather rachis.

Figure 4.10
Quilled roach feather with ermine & marabou fluff additions.

Figure 4.11
Detail of quilled section with ermine & fluff decoration.

Carefully pull away the marabou vane from one side of the fluff just as you would for stripping a wing feather. Secure one end of the strip to the feather with a few wraps of waxed string or sinew. Smear a thin layer of craft glue along the area to be wrapped with the marabou strip. Using the spring-tweezers to gently grasp the other end of the feather to hold it taught and guide it in place. Spin the main feather while guiding the marabou in place over the glued section.

Adding a strip of marabou in this manner works well when the main feather being decorated is going to be viewed from all sides like a roach feather. The example feather was created with such a use in mind, a roach feather of distinction.

Slide the tip of a flattened quill under the standing line and fold it over the standing line, covering the inserted tip, and wrap around the rachis (see **Figure 4.12**). Loop the quill over the fastening line with the quill end next to the rachis. Tie a half-hitch around the standing line with the fastening line (see **Figure 4.13**). As the fastening line is drawn tight the string pulls the quill tight around the feather rachis. An awl tip can be used to push the end of the quill under the main body of the quill as it is drawn up tight by drawing down on the half-hitch of the fastening line. Continue adding one quill after another for the length of the section to be quilled. Secure the finishing line with a series of half-hitches on the standing line. A small dab of glue is also useful.

Figure 4.13
Fold quill over fastening line & make half-hitch around standing line. Pull tight to secure quill.

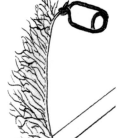

Figure 4.14
Fold quill over fastening line & make half-hitch around standing line. Pull tight to secure quill.

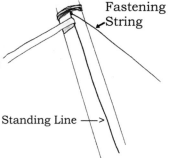

Fastening String

Standing Line ⟶

Figure 4.12
Quill inserted under standing line and folded over itself to begin wrapping around feather rachis.

As seen in the photos, fur and feathers are used at either end of the quilled section to hide the wrappings of the waxed string. The distal end has a thin segment of ermine fur glued in place. The proximal end has a stripped vane of fluff wrapped around and glued in place. The stripped vane of a fluff is another interesting way to dress-up your feathers.

Figure 4.15
Detail view of finished seam.

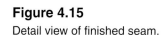

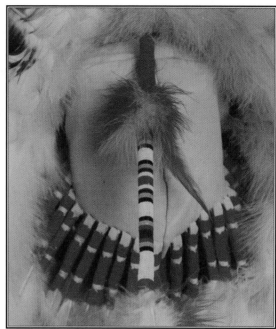

Close-up Photos of Warbonnet Decorations

Upper Left: Wrappings of the side-drop feathers on the war bonnet.

Upper Right: Bead wrapped and decorated major plume of the war bonnet.

Right: Conch shell disc used as a medallion, wrapped bases on feather drops and beaded brow band with small hawk bell adornment.

Below: Base wrappings of the main feathers on the war bonnet.

Crazy Crow Trading Post Photos.

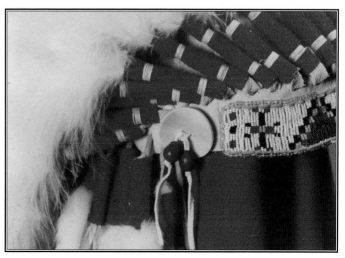

Northern Plains Style Bonnet
This magnificent bonnet was created by Mike Tucker, using hand painted feathers and plumes, horsehair, and ermine skins.
Photo courtesy of Mike Tucker.

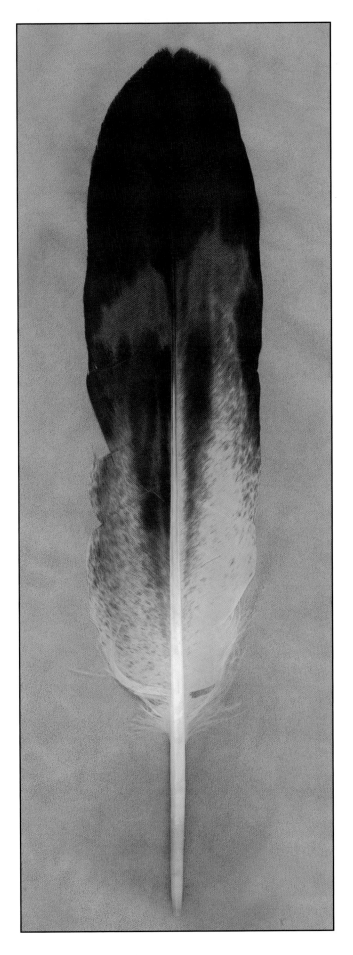

Chapter 5

Feather Projects

Once one has mastered the techniques of creating a single raptor feather, each finished feather is a testament to the artisans' creativity and artistic style. Inherent in such accomplishment is an intrinsic value which bestows upon the artisan a sense of well-earned pride and achievement. The production of a single masterpiece, or even several hundred of such, is not the epitome of the art of feather craft. Of greater virtue is the employment of such individual creations in the sculpting of an artifact whose inherent beauty and aesthetic value is greater than the sum of the parts. An entirely new set of skills must be learned, cultivated and nurtured in order to create such feather crafts.

This chapter's focus is the application of the skills presented in previous chapters to projects which employ feathers, both raptor reproductions and natural mimics. The instructions given may be a bit brief at times due to an assumption that you have already read through the detailed instructions of a particular technique in a previous chapter. Please refer back to **Chapters 3: Feather Alteration** and **4: Feather Adornment** for detailed instructions of specific skills. Within these project notes may be found some new feather craft techniques that may be unique to the project presented and so are introduced here as opposed to the general skills and techniques presented in previous chapters.

This chapter is dedicated to the introduction of such skills necessary for utilizing the feathers in a variety of projects which employ a multitude of skills and techniques. What is presented herein is not meant to be a definitive nor exhaustive compilation of feather-craft techniques. What you will discover are helpful tips, tricks and techniques that I have found useful while employing my raptor reproductions and mimics in a variety of artifacts commonly seen among the pow-wow world and Native American artifacts.

Indubitably I expect many responses to this section of the book in-particular as many readers may have alternative methods of using feathers. Let it be known that such feedback from readers is wholeheartedly welcomed. Without such an open flow of knowledge this book would never have been possible. Many excellent artisans and historians have shared their knowledge with me and it is that same spirit of sharing that ignited the spark of an idea for this very book. Until all those wonderful suggestions are compiled in the future to warrant another edition, let the instructions of the following pages act as a primer to the artistry of feather craft.

Gray Hawk, Teton Sioux
This man was an informant for Frances Densmore in "Teton Sioux Music", 1915. His bonnet consists of black & white eagle tail feathers with small hawk feathers and ribbons used as side drops.

Northern Plains Style Bonnet

No other singular artifact of the Native Americans is more recognized and associated with native culture than the eagle feather bonnet.

Depictions of native peoples in film, on stage and even in cartoon form have cemented the association of the eagle feather 'warbonnet' with the Indigenous Nations of North America. While this certainly wasn't a complete untruth it wasn't always entirely historically accurate either. Colin Taylor has written an extensive treatise on the history of the feathered bonnet and very clearly illustrates the differences in style and construction between tribes. (*Wapa'ha: The Plains Feathered Head-dress,* © *1994*) Dr. Taylor explains that many tribes had variations of the feathered head-dress in early history but later adopted the flaring eagle tail feather bonnet as it became, even among Native Americans, a symbol of Native American culture. As such, this section will focus on the construction techniques employed in creating the flaring style, eagle tail feather bonnet with a few notations on distinguishing tribal characteristics interjected.

Sequence of Construction

Prepare all main feathers with extensions and/or loops, base and tip decoration and cut bridle lace slit through ventral rachis.

Create cap or make adjustments for size to a pre-made felt cap, mark eagle feather locations and cut slits for lacing thong.

Sew brow band in place, mark main feather locations around perimeter.

Attach major plume at apex of crown and sew crown covering materials in place.

Attach eagle feathers to crown with leather lace through each loop.

Thread bridle string through each feather and adjust to get desired shape of bonnet.

Attach side drop decorations.

Begin your bonnet project, as one does with any other, by collecting all necessary materials. Historic specimens of bonnets include anywhere from 18-42 eagle feathers (not including trailer feathers suspended from the back of a bonnet). Considering that most reproductions available are a bit smaller in length and width than real eagle tails twenty will mostly likely be too few so thirty-two feathers is a good average. Purchase or paint a few extra to make sure you have enough to choose from in selecting the largest and widest feathers possible, selecting sixteen rights and sixteen lefts. Another consideration is the use of reproductions made from spliced turkey primary feathers as presented in **Chapter 3.**

Other materials needed are skull cap material, material for covering the feather base, rawhide for feather loops, sinew (imitation if preferred), fluffs and/or horsehair for feather base and tip decoration, feathers or fur for temple dangles, brow band materials, steam iron, scissors, sharp knife, awl, and needles of various sizes. This is just a general list of tools and materials. Material needs will vary depending on the specific design aspects of your bonnet.

Once you have shaped, trimmed, and sorted your feathers you will need to add the rawhide loops to the base of each feather. Rawhide is specifically mentioned because a stiff loop wrapped closely to the end of the calamus will better hold the feathers in place than a flimsy leather loop with lots of 'play'. Wrapping a broad, flat piece of stiff rawhide onto a round feather calamus presents a problem. A simple and historically accurate solution is to iron the calamus flat so that it is flattened in the same plane as the vanes of the feather (see **Figure 5.1**). Use plenty of steam from a hot iron to soften the calamus as you iron it flat. Be careful not to burn yourself or the feather.

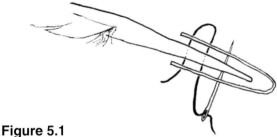

Figure 5.1
Sewing rawhide onto flattened calamus of bonnet feather.

The sketch to the right shows the finished loop sewn in place. As mentioned previously, the reproduction eagle feathers available are generally smaller than real eagle feathers necessitating an extension piece. One can extend the feather and still have a flattened feather quill to affix the rawhide slat by using a feather quill as the extension piece. White turkey feathers bought in bulk or wild turkey feathers are inexpensive enough to obtain enough extra to cut the calamus from one feather in order to affix it to your bonnet feather.

[For lack of a better term, let us refer to the extension piece as the 'scrap' feather in the following directions.] Strip the vanes from the scrap feather and trim the remaining rachis to a length

of about 4-5 inches (11.25-12.5 cm). Cut the calamus of the bonnet feather to expose the hollow shaft. Insert the scrap rachis section into the hollow shaft of the bonnet feather and glue in place. It may be necessary to carefully shave down the rachis to allow it to fit better. An extension of 2-2.5 inches (4-5 cm) is generally all one would need to get an eagle-sized feather of 14-15 inches (35-37.5 cm) long. If you've managed to get a nice set of long, wide feathers in the 12-13 inch (30-32.5 cm) range, you may not need the feather extensions to produce a beautiful bonnet, but the choice is yours.

Figure 5.2
Completed stitching of rawhide loop on flattened calamus of bonnet feather.

This extension process should be completed first. After all the bonnet feathers have had extensions added, trim the feathers to the desired length by cutting a section of the new extension. Lay the feathers in a row with the feather tips along a straight line. The quill ends will be of different lengths at this point. Mark the quills along a straight line and trim so that each feather will now be the same length. If you've extended the feathers you may have plenty of extra quill to remove.

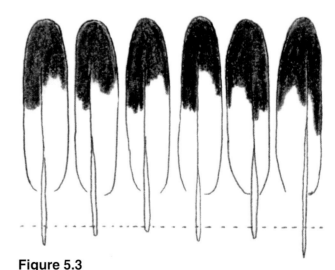

Figure 5.3
Line up feathers along the top edge so they will be even in the final project. Cut the quills along a straight line using the shortest feather as the gauge for all the feathers. (shown as dotted line in sketch) This works for setting bonnet & bustle feather sets.

War bonnet made of standard, dyed imitation eagle feathers. This illustrates how good technique and attention to detail can enhance the available materials. *Crazy Crow Trading Post Photo.*

At this point you should have your feathers sorted into rights and lefts, extended (if necessary), trimmed to the same length, the calamus flattened, a slit through the ventral rachis for the bridle thong, and the rawhide loops sewn in place. Work from the bottom up to finish each feather. Common decorations of bonnet feathers include a red wool 'firecracker' with fluffs emerging from beneath the wool at the base of the vanes. The feather tip usually has horsehair or feather fluff affixed to the tip under a white leather or ermine fur spot or a small mound of gypsum. Gypsum and curly cow tail hair are common among museum specimens.

With the feathers prepared, the next step is to assemble the crown onto which the feathers will be strung. Pre-made felt and wool skull caps are available from several craft suppliers and are quite historically accurate. Many bonnets of the late 19th and early 20th century were made from the felt crown of hats after the brim had been removed. When caps were made of leather, a simple, three-panel design was common. As **Figure 5.4** illustrates there is a rectangular section that runs front to back with a semicircle piece sewn along each side. The catalog card notations of several bonnets in the Smithsonian's National Museum of Natural History indicate a cotton cloth lining on the inner and outer surfaces of the skull cap.

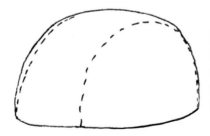

Figure 5.4
Completed stitching of rawhide loop on flattened calamus of bonnet feather.

Use a cloth measuring tape to take three different head measurements of the wearer; (A) from just above the eyebrows to the back of the head where the cervical vertebrae attach to the skull; (B) from just above one ear up and over the top of the head to just above the other ear; (C) the circumference of the head, keeping the tape just above the eyebrows and the tops of the ears. [Add in a quarter of an inch (1cm) to each measurement to make sure the cap is not too snug.] The rectangular section is measurement A by 4 inches (10 cm) wide. The widths of each semicircle along the bottom are measurement C, minus 8 inches (20cm), and then divide the remainder in half. For example, if the head circumference is 22 inches, subtract 8 inches to get 14 inches and divided in half to get 7 inches for the width. (55.8cm − 20.3cm = 35.5cm/2 = 17.75 cm) The height of the semicircle would be measurement B minus 4 inches and divided in half. After marking these measurements of width and height on a heavy paper template, a compass can be used to create the arch and connect the dots. The length of the arc should be equal to measurement A in order to match up with the rectangular section when sewn together. Make a practice cap out of scrap material before cutting into your best brain-tanned leather. Proper planning will help in placing the feathers properly around the circumference of the cap. Divide the circumference of the cap by the number of feathers to determine how far apart to place the feathers. [e.g. 24 in/32 feathers = 0.75 inches (61 cm/32 = 1.9 cm)] Fold the bonnet in half to mark the center point in front and back with a pencil or chalk (never use ink on leather, it can't be erased like pencil and chalk). From this center point on front begin to mark off each feather's location before cutting the holes in the cap for the leather thong that will hold each feather in place. It's helpful to sew on your brow band before marking the feather placements. If those two front feathers are to be 3/4 inches apart, half of that would 3/8 inches. Measure 3/8 of an inch to each side of the center line to have the location of the two front feathers. Starting with these two feather points, measure and mark lines 3/4 of an inch apart around the circumference of the cap. These lines are the actual locations of each feather so we next mark the location of where to cut slits to run the lacing thong through the rawhide loops to attach the feathers. If the rawhide loop is 1/4 wide then the distance between the two slits for each feather should be 1/4 of an inch. Half of that distance is 1/8 of an inch. So, measure 1/8 of an inch on either side of each initial feather marking around the bonnet. A useful tip shared by Bob Laidig was to use white masking tape to mark your feather placement around the skull cap. Cut each strip of tape as wide as the rawhide loop at the base of the feather. As you place the tape strips around the cap you visually see exactly where each feather will be located prior to making any cuts. You can shuffle the tape sections around the cap to make sure the feathers have the proper placement. Keep in mind that the figures given thus far are for our example bonnet and may not match your measurements.

As indicated in the diagram below, there are certain considerations when making your feather marks around the circumference of the cap. Around the front of the bonnet the feathers are positioned above the brow band, but as the feathers flow around to the back they follow a lower line on the cap. This shift in placement helps flare the feathers. On either side of the head, at the temple area, the line of feathers drop from just above the brow band down to half an inch (1.5 cm) up from the caps edge. Notice that as the slits for the feathers drop from higher to lower line they keep their distance of three-quarters of an inch (2cm) and the lacing thong slits are cut at a slight angle instead of being perpendicular to the caps edge. To help guide this visual effect of the feathers flowing from one line to another one can use tail feathers from nearer the outer edge of the tail. These feathers have a slight curve at the superior umbilicus and thinner leading edge vane so they will give the visual appearance of curving toward the back of the bonnet naturally at this point.

This area of transition of the bonnet feathers is also the area of attachment of side drops. Of the forty National Museum of Natural History catalog cards I reviewed, twenty-three noted side drop features. Colored ribbons and ermine skins were most common decorations with fifteen of the twenty-three noted bonnets having ribbons, ermine or both. Hawk feathers were the next most common decorative materials. Along with material hanging down there is generally an item placed just above the placement of the drops. Common decorations include quilled wheels, rawhide cut-outs, abalone shell disk, and beaded rosettes. Perhaps the most unique decoration noted in the NMNH collection was beaded reptile figurines on either side of the head. Another unique piece is artifact 50/3082 at the American Museum of Natural History which has the full leg of a Golden Eagle with foot attached tied onto the bonnet at this location.

Several references describe the covering of the main portion of the skull cap with feather fluffs or fur strips. It is not entirely clear how common this is on historic examples, pre-1900, as many museum specimens are photographed or displayed with only a front view available. Of the forty NMNH catalog cards mentioned previously, only four mention such a crown covering. Two have ermine fur, one has hawk feathers and the last has red and yellow dyed fluffs. One should also take into account the use of cloth coverings over the felt or leather cap material. There were a half a dozen bonnets with canvas, blue calico or silk ribbon coverings noted in the records. Plate 55 of the *1911 Annual Bulletin of the Bureau of Ethnology* does show a bonnet from the rear and it is covered in colored fluff feathers. The Cheyenne Chief White Eagle's bonnet in the collection of the AMNH (item 502/1182A) has the head of a hawk with nape feathers covering the bonnet crown. Despite its questionable popularity among historic examples it is probably safe to say that crown coverings are a common feature of the modern feathered bonnet.

Applying fluffs or ermine strips (white rabbit is a good substitute for ermine) to the crown is a simple process. Attach a single thread to the cap and begin making back-stitches in concentric circles around the crown. Each time you take a back-stitch a loop is created in the thread that, when pulled taught to the cap, will hold the fluff or fur strip in place. Keep the crown covering higher on the crown so that it is not seen between the main eagle feathers once they are attached around the perimeter (see **Figure 5.5**, previous page).

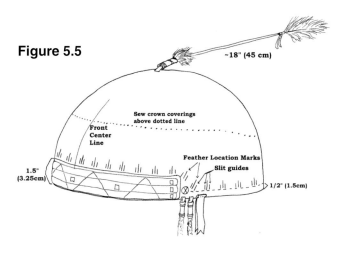

Figure 5.5

Another design element to the flared feather bonnet that is easy to overlook is the major plume. This long shaft extends back from the apex of the crown and is generally not seen from the front of the bonnet. While the popularity of crown feathers is uncertain in historical examples, records show that the major plume, or some other decoration centrally located, was commonly employed. To create such a quill, strip the vanes off a primary wing feather and decorate the quill in any of a variety of ways that suits you. Generally, the tip of the stripped rachis has a bundle of fluffs or an extra-large eagle plume attached which, of course, gives this piece its descriptive name. The remainder of the rachis can be quilled, beaded, thread-wrapped, dyed/painted, wrapped in ribbon, etc. Many museum pieces indicate colorful feathers in pink, purple, green, red, yellow, blue, and black feathers along with the end plumes. **Figure 5.6** illustrates three methods of attaching for the major plume to the apex of the skull cap.

Figure 5.6

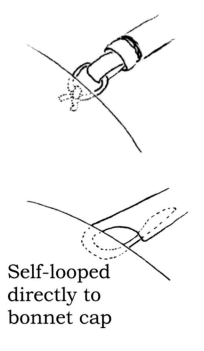

Heavy leather disk sewn to cap

Leather string bound to calamus & woven through holes in disk

Self-looped directly to bonnet cap

Once the main bonnet feathers are in place you need to weave the bridle thong through each feather. Using a sharp knife carefully cut a transverse slit four to five inches up from the bottom of the feather through the ventral rachis in much the same manner as you would when preparing bustle feathers. A leather lace works well as it fills the slit in the ventral rachis and keeps the feathers in place once you set them. A little glue on the end of the lace will firm it up like a needle to aide in passing the thong through each slit. Start at the center feather at the front of the bonnet and work back each side. Space the feathers evenly along the lace as you progress from the front around each side to the back. Once you've got them all connected you can try on the bonnet to check the positioning of the feathers. Adjustments can be made to tighten the bridle strand to pull the feathers up together more or loosen them to get more flare as you see fit.

Leather laces are sometimes added at the temples to tie the bonnet on. If you plan to be involved in active events while wearing your bonnet this may be a good addition.

If your feathers around the front of the crown have a tendency to lay back more than you'd like there is a simple and effective method of maneuvering the feathers upright. Cut a segment of leather or cloth, preferably of the same material of your bonnet skull cap, approximately four inches by ten inches. Tightly roll this segment so that you have a ten inch length of dense cordage. Stitch this roll into place behind the front feathers and the skull cap as shown in the sketch to the right.

By using the same material as the skull cap this roll will be less obvious when viewed from the front.

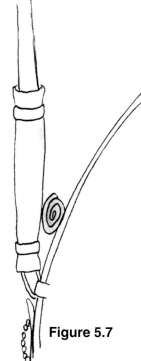

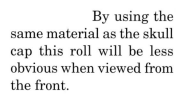
Figure 5.7

Two Shields, Teton Sioux
Consisting of a large, black & white eagle tail feathers, this rather unusual bonnet stands up much higher than normal and sports the additional decoration of small hawk bells between the bases of each feather.

Red Fox (Tokala-Iu'ta), Oglala Sioux
This man's warbonnet is very simply decorated, with an unusually long beaded brow band and multiple ribbon side drops. He became a warrior at a very young age, as he explained in "Teton Sioux Music" and he was a leader with the first Oglala delegation to Washington in 1870.

Double Trailer Bonnet
This huge, double trailer bonnet contains approximately 140 immature golden eagle tail feathers. The beaded brow band is a simple design but quite wide, and the trailer feathers appear to be mounted on red Stroud cloth.

63

Two modern war bonnets with hand-painted imitation eagle feathers. *Photo by Crazy Crow Trading Post.*

Modern style warbonnet with hand painted feathers, lazy stitch brow band, rabbit fur and ribbon side drops, and a pink conch shell on each side used as a medallion. *Photo by Crazy Crow Trading Post.*

Gerald Chasenah, Comanche, is wearing a large, finely constructed war bonnet of hand painted imitation eagle feathers, with a beaded brow band and rabbit fur side drops. *Photo by Ginger Otipoby Reddick.*

This frontal view of the above war bonnet illustrates the "flare" that is common in bonnets from the Central Plains area. *Photo by Crazy Crow Trading Post.*

Feathered Hair Decorations

Women dancer's of the pow-wow circuit today wear feathers in their hair that can dance and flutter along with them as they dip, shuffle, shimmy and twirl around the dance arbor. At the back of the head, projecting skyward is the large plume with lots of plumaceous marabou. The plumes are often held in place by a large, beaded barrette. To facilitate these feathers being held in place it's better to create a single piece of adornment instead of several, individual feathers.

Cut two sections of leather of appropriate size to be hidden discreetly beneath the barrette worn at the back of the head. Smear a light layer of glue on one piece of leather and lay the feather quills in place in the glue. The dorsal side of the feathers faces backwards, away from the head so someone dancing behind you would see the top of the feather. Add some glue to the top side of the feather quills and press the top piece of leather in place. Lay a heavy item on the glued section while it dries to ensure good adhesion. While this is certainly a quick and simple method of construction, there are alternative methods that require a little more time to complete but they are more secure methods of holding the feathers in place and add a little flare at the same time.

Positioning the feathers between two pieces of leather is still standard but instead of just glue, stitch the edge of the leather segments together including the short segment between each feather. The stitches between the feathers will hold them in just the right position. Beads between the feathers, strung on a waxed string like a bridle string of a bustle, will also hold the feathers in position. These bridle strings and beads can be hidden beneath the leather covering.

Similar to the tail section of a crow bustle, a rawhide piece can be folded in half with holes along the fold through which the feathers can project upwards (see **Figure 5.8**). Thin rawhide will work sufficiently to secure the feathers in place and position them the desired distance from each other and still be flexible enough to fit comfortably under the barrette. The rawhide could also be painted after a fashion of the old parfleche containers for a unique and attractive alternative to the beaded barrette.

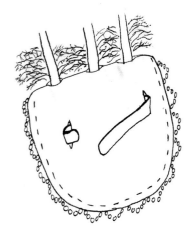

Figure 5.8
Back-side of beaded barrette with plumes inserted in the fold. Metal barrette slid through slits in the leather.

Additionally, glue or stitch leather over top of the rawhide and apply beadwork or quillwork directly to the leather covering. This melds the beadwork decoration with the feather decorations so you only have one piece of jewelry to attach instead of two separate pieces. This of course requires the addition of the metal barrette directly to the rawhide and leather holding.

Some simple stitches looping over the metal backing of the barrette and through the leather can work fine. Alternatively, cut two slits in the backing material and slide the metal barrette through the material.

Wearing feathers in the hair that hang down the side of your head is also a very common decoration with dancers today. There is a very simple method of attachment with the help of a barrette.

Begin by adding a leather thong off the end of each feather. You can add in some colored feather fluffs and finish with decorative thread-wrapping over the leather slice. On the opposite end of the leather thong one can add another bit of decoration like a tin cone with horsehair tuft. Of course, you could also just add another axillary feather to match the first one.

As **Figure 5.9** indicates, the simple method of clamping the leather thongs within the barrette when attaching it your hair. Keep the distance between the feathered ends to a minimum so the feathers don't get too out of control while you're dancing. And, just in case you're thinking this technique only applies to women I would suggest that a guy could use this as well. Just choose a very simply designed barrette in a color that closely matches your hair color and no one will notice it under those fluttering feathers.

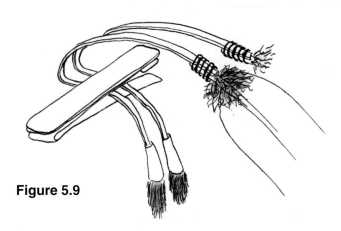

Figure 5.9

`Another technique that is a bit more specialized for male dancers is the attachment of feathers to a roach. More specifically, the feathers are attached to your scalplock braid used for attaching your roach, or strings used for tying your roach in place as the case may be.

A loop of leather at the bottom of the feather cluster or pair of feathers set together is all one needs. Pass your braid through the leather loop before snaking your braid up through the hole in your roach base.

If you're setting a pair of feathers together in such a way that you want the feathers to hold their position like a fan set instead of fluttering clusters, prepare the feathers in the same manner as a bustle set. You can loop the ends of the feathers and add a bridle string with bead separators to keep the feathers in position. I have a set of axillary feathers that I set in this manner and it has served me well for over ten years of dancing.

Old-Style Bustles

The category of 'old-style' bustle contains such a vast and diverse array of dance bustles employed by a number of tribes throughout the prairie and plains regions of North America from the early 19th through mid-20th centuries. Attempting to present a full compliment of the varieties of old-style dance bustle would be as overwhelming as categorizing the thousands of species of beetles that inhabit the Earth. Considering this, presented here are just two examples of old-style bustles with accompanying instructions for each to provide some ideas that may germinate plans for your own bustle.

Our first example was inspired by a Sioux Crow belt in the American Museum of Natural History. The simplistic design of this bustle is indicative of the earlier incarnations of the 'crow belt' dance bustle from the early- to mid-19th century.

The main component is a 5"x12" section of buffalo rawhide (hair on) folded in half with a 'trailer' made from a whole, natural horsetail. The skin of the tail has been split and folded open. The horse tail was freeze-dried by tacking the wet tail out on a board in the dead of winter. This results in a slightly more flexible rawhide.

Prior to folding the buffalo rawhide in half, the horse tail was attached to the backside, interior of the buffalo section. A battery operated drill is a less-than-traditional but highly effective tool for creating holes in the rawhide tail and base section.

With the tail attached, the buffalo section was folded in half and sinew-stitched along four inches (10 cm) of each edge to hold it closed. By not sewing up the sides completely, the folded rawhide creates a loop through which one can pass a belt for wearing the bustle.

Instead of a wheel of feathers attached to the face of the bustle base, this version has two eagle wing spikes which lay down in front of the bustle. The spikes (painted turkey wing primaries) have been extended five inches to approximate the actual length of an eagle feather which runs from about 18 to 21 inches (46-54 cm). These extensions are concealed beneath the stockade of secondary owl wing feathers (reproductions) and great-horned owl contour feathers (mimics). The wing feathers are self-spliced, strung onto a brain-tan lace and wound around the base of the spike. Small contour feathers of this type do not require leather loops for stringing and are held in place by wrapped sinew thread. The use of real sinew has many advantages and is recommended especially on reproduction pieces of this type.

Covering the various wrappings at the base of the spike is a section of brain-tanned hide sewn in place. Leather thongs remain at the base of the spikes for attaching the spikes to the rawhide base. The tie thongs are simply passed through holes in the base and tied together in the back. At the tip of each spike is a short section of horsehair dyed red and held in place with sinew. A common adornment of old-style bustle spikes is the addition of small, hawk bells along the length of the spike. These can be individually tied along the ventral rachis or attached as a strand of bells that stretches from the base to the tip.

The horsetail trailer is decorated with ten eagle secondary wing feathers (reproductions). Each feather is self-looped and wrapped with sinew. For attachment to the tail, a leather thong is tied to the feather loop using a sheet-bend.

66

Sinew is used to splice the leather thong to strands of the horsehair. Tight wraps around the leather and horsehair together hold the feather firmly in place. Here again we see the virtue of real sinew. As the moist sinew dries after wrapping, it shrinks and tightens even more to secure the feather in the horsetail.

Figure 5.11
Leather thong attached with sheet bend to feather quill.

Figure 5.10
 This diagramatic sketch shows the basic construction design and feather attachment points. See color photo of completed bustle below.

On the bottom corners of the buffalo base are clusters of three rough-legged hawk tail feathers. Each feather has been self-looped, the loop secured with sinew, and then attached as a cluster with a heavy sinew thread. Alongside the base, attached directly to the elk leather strap serving as a belt, are falcon primary and sub-adult, Golden Eagle secondary wing feathers (reproductions). This technique was inspired by several museum examples which have feathers attached to the belt proper as well as the bustle base or trailer.

Figure 5.12   Sioux Crow Belt with horsetail trailer.

The next bustle presented, shown below, employs what may be considered more 'typical' design elements of old-style bustles, namely; rawhide base, upright spikes, central feather wheel, center rosette, tail segment, and cloth trailer.

The base is a rawhide section folded in half and stitched with sinew along three sides as shown in **Figure 5.14**. There are several historic examples of rawhide bases filled with buffalo wool or feathers like a pillow but the example shown is of elk rawhide only. (see **Figure 5.14**) Two holes are burned through the center with a hot nail to allow the passage of two strings attached to the center rosette. These strings also then hold all the concentric rings of feathers that make up the main body of the bustle, the feather wheel (see **Figure 5.19**). In the upper left and right corners are T-cuts into which the bases of the spikes are inserted (see **Figure 5.15**). Holes can be burned along the bottom edge of the base for attaching the cloth trailer and tail section.

Figure 5.14
Simplified sketch of old-style bustle components of base, tail section, main and secondary trailers and spikes with stockade feathers at base.

Figure 5.15
This sketch shows alternatives to the T-cut for spike attachment. Historical examples include the T-cut (far left), U-cut (center), and I-cut (right).

Each spike consists of two primary wing spikes wrapped within a fur covering. At the tip are immature Golden Eagle tail coverts and some immature Bald Eagle contour feathers held in place with sinew wrappings and red ribbon. The base of the spike is decorated with bundles of feathers, known as stockades. The stockades on this bustle contain Great Horned Owl wing feathers stripped, parried and dyed orange, magpie and kestrel wing feathers dyed red. While several historical pieces I've handled had no tie strings for the spikes, these spikes are secured to the base with a leather lace in much the same fashion as illustrated in **Figure 5.10**. Stacking multiple primary wing quills can be awkward as they're rounded. By ironing flat the calamus from tip to the superior umbilicus one can more easily layer the feathers for spikes. (see **Figure 5.16**)

Figure 5.13   Old style bustle.

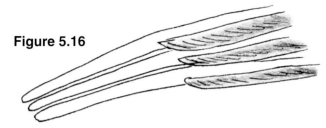

Figure 5.16

A key element to old-style bustles is the tail attached to the bottom of the base. The tail is a section of Golden Eagle tail feathers, generally five, set into a piece of rawhide which is then attached to the bottom of the rawhide base. Certainly there is a wide variety of old-style bustles but other authorities who have studied bustles found that at least 95% of the museum specimens investigated contained a tail segment. **Figure 5.18** indicates the rawhide piece used in attaching the tail. Make X cuts as indicated along the center line and insert the calamus of the feather. Glue feathers in place as you fold the rawhide in half and sew along each side. The holes are for attaching the tail to the base (see **Figure 5.17**, holes marked letter B).

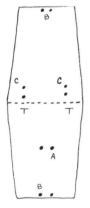

Figure 5.17
Bustle base of rawhide, fold on dotted line. T-cuts indicate spike position. A is for attachment of feather wheel. Tail segment attaches at point B. Cloth or leather loops at C will hold belt for tying bustle around waist. Dimensions: 14 in. long, 7 in. wide at center, 6 in. wide at each end.

Cloth trailers on old-style bustles can be found as single, wide sections or two, thinner strips or a combination of each. Our example displays a wide trailer covered in over 40 Cooper's hawk tail feathers. Each feather has had a leather loop added and they are attached in rows of six feathers over the trailer. A leather lace runs from the back side of the trailer to the front side through a small slit, is run through the loop of a feather and back through the same slit. The blue wool has had a calico backing hand-stitched in place after the addition of the feathers and finished by hand-stitching ribbon around the edge. The exemplar bustle also has a second set of trailers which contain small, sub-adult Golden Eagle wing feathers. These secondary trailers are four inch strips of wool attached to the rawhide base near the top of the base. Many museum specimens indicate the attachment of double trailers nearer the top of the rawhide base than at the bottom.

The main focus of the old-style bustle is the center feather wheel. This consists of concentric rings of feathers strung together in layers of feathers with each ring of feathers being its own unique work of art that contributes to the overall artifacts brilliance. A leather or rawhide cone at the bottom of the feather layers helps form the feather cluster into a bowl shape that projects away from the body. Several museum pieces do not use a leather cone but simply have a flat, rawhide disc between the feather wheel and the bustle base. The feathers can also be shaped into a cone or bowl-shaped by adjusting the tension of the bridle string. Leave less space between the feathers and they won't flatten but will hold their cone shape.

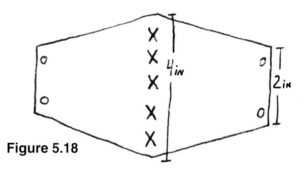

Figure 5.18

Figure 5.19 indicates the layers of concentric feather rings strung along the tie thong. Rosettes can be anything from rawhide cutouts (sometimes painted), to layers of ribbon, a metal concho or mirror or even a piece of costume jewelry from the early 20th century.

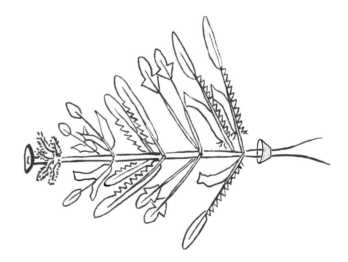

Figure 5.19
Stringing concentric rings of feathers for the feathered wheel of old-style bustles. See **Figure 5.35** for details of making a rawhide cone for the wheel.

Each feather of each ring has been self-looped at the base for stringing together. A bridle string of cotton thread or imitation sinew will help keep the feathers spread equidistantly in a ring. Beads or other spacers aren't necessary since the bridle string isn't a design element like those of contemporary bustles. Simply loop the bridle string around each feather by going through the ventral side of the rachis with needle and string then going back through the same hole (see **Figure 5.20**). This can be loosened as needed to slide a feather in either direction but cinched down again to hold the feather in place.

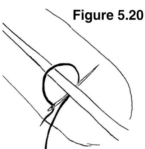

Figure 5.20   As the illustration of **Figure 5.19** indicates, the feathers of each ring have been altered in some way to add to the visual aesthetics of the feather wheel. This bustle includes the following feather rings, from the center outward: owl body feathers (mimics) & hawk underwing coverts dyed yellow (reproductions), immature Bald Eagle wing coverts (reproductions), Ferruginous hawk tails (mimics), 2 rings of stripped & parried hawk wings (reproductions), eagle secondary wings stripped, parried & trimmed (reproductions), and hawk primary spikes stripped, serrated, tipped with yellow plume and the addition of a stripped section of falcon wing feather dyed red spliced onto the base of each hawk primary (reproductions). While most of the feathers of this bustle have the dorsal side facing outward, away from the dancer, many historic pieces have feathers with the ventral side facing outward.

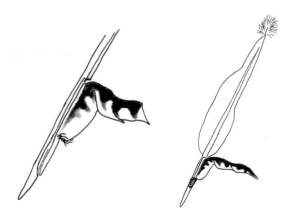

Figure 5.21   Old style bustle. These sketches show how I modified the hawk primary feathers with a section of dyed falcon primary stripped & excised from the rachis. Excised falcon section sinew-wrapped to base of hawk primary for added 3-D effect. Bustle primaries are stripped on one side & serrated on the other.

Once again, the old-style bustles presented are just two versions of a plethora of styles and designs and the techniques employed in their creation. Designs and styles vary from tribe to tribe and temporally, having a number of manifestations over time. The following are additional suggestions to aid you in your planning and embellishing of an old-style bustle. Most of these techniques come from vintage bustles.

Additional Feathers and Techniques

Rawhide cutout effigies tied onto the bustle trailer. Examples include pointed stars, round disks with serrated edges, various birds and mammals, and lightning bolts. Rawhide effigies have also been noted on the main 'body' of bustles. Rawhide stars can also be added at the point of attachment of the spikes.

Rawhide bases cut with bird effigies along top edge

Woven strands hanging from the belt proper with an assortment of feathers attached along the length of the woven strands.

Sections of bird skin attached to the front of the rawhide base. Eagle, hawk, crow and raven are used in historic examples but a facsimile can be created by airbrushing a section of white goose, chicken or turkey hide. There are also naturally colored geese, chickens and turkeys that one could use to get a similar appearance. Several museum specimens have entire crow skins attached to them. Alice Fletcher reported that the Omaha attached a full crow skin to the left side of the "Crow." (*27th Annual Bulletin of the Bureau of Ethnology, 1911; p. 441*)

Netted wheels with feather attachments have been recorded as decorations of the body of the bustle as well as along the edge of bustle (and bonnet) trailers. These netted wheels are smaller versions (~3 inches, 7.5cm) of the netted hoops used in the hoop & stick game. In common parlance they might be called 'dreamcatchers' but as these items were not necessarily assembled and attached to the bustles for the purposes purported by the 'legend' of the dreamcatcher, the term netted wheel seems more apropos.

Quilled strips along the length of the shafts of the feathers of the tail segment.

In the later part of the 19th century, it was fashionable to have three feather wheels in a bustle. Each wheel was about 12-14 inches (30-35 cm) in diameter. They were set with two bustles on the bottom line with one centered over these two to create a triangle. Such bustles did not always have cloth trailers.

An excellent O'Neill photo capturing these Old Time Sioux outfits in great detail. Caption reads *"South Dakota Indian War Dancers."* Courtesy of the **Smithsonian Institution, Washington, D.C.** #55901.

The photo caption reads *"Indian War Dancers, O'Neill Photo I-16."* These dancers have incorporated a multitude of feathers into their Grass Dance outfits. Courtesy of the **Smithsonian Institution, Washington, D.C.** #55902.

The use of three primary spikes (numbers 1, 2, & 3) as the main spikes of the bustle without any covering material. The differing lengths of feathers create an interesting, three-dimensional aspect to the spikes as shown in **Figure 5.22**. Another variation of the spikes is to strip the vanes from the primary spikes leaving two or three inches of vane near the tip where small feathers, fluffs, furs, or ribbons can be attached. The positioning of the spikes also differed from different bustle styles over time. Spikes can hang down in front as seen in **Figure 5.10,** protrude at right angles to the base or stand erect from the base as seen in **Figure 5.14.**

Figure 5.22

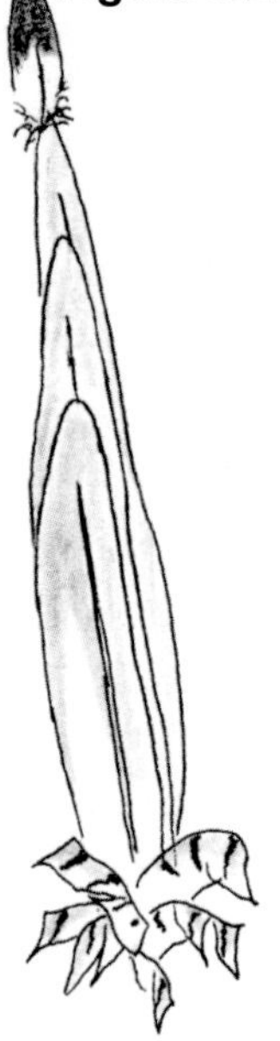

Along the length of the bare spikes tie ½ inch hawk bells directly to the rachis or wrap a long strand of hawk bells around the length of the spike in a spiral.

Rawhide 'horns' affixed to base to jut out at right angles from the base.

Employ a 4" wide sash, woven, in lieu of the rawhide base and attach feathers and spikes directly to the sash. Spikes will hang down loosely, not stand erect. Sew cloth trailers to the bottom edge of the sash where they will be positioned at your back.

Tie a wolf's tail to the lower corner of the base or from the belt at a position next to the base. A number of museum specimens include this adornment and Alice Fletcher has reported the Omaha added a wolf's tail to the right side of the "Crow." (*27th Annual Bulletin of the Bureau of Ethnology, 1911; p. 441*) As wolf's tails may be a difficult acquisition, one may find a coyote tail a fine substitute. It should also be noted that the term wolf in the reference materials is not specified as Canus lupus. It is possible that the tail employed originally was, entirely or in part, the coyote, Canis latrans. I have noted several incidents of misidentification of animal and bird parts on museum specimens as well as the simple lack of distinction between similar species. For example, several authors of Anthropological Papers use the terms crow and raven interchangeably when these birds are distinctly different species. There is also little evidence of distinction between similar species of mammal and bird within the native languages.

For further study of old-style bustles search museum online databases at,
BeuchelMuseum: *http://www.sfmission.org/museum/American Museum of Natural History: http://anthro.amnh.org/*

Contemporary Traditional Bustle

The example shown in **Figure 5.23** is a basic swing bustle of immature Golden Eagle tail feathers. To construct a contemporary swing bustle, begin by sorting your feathers into rights and lefts. Lay the feathers on a table in the order in which you want them in the bustle. Begin with the feathers near the top and lay each successive feather on top of the one before it so that a feathers' leading edge is overlaying the trailing edge of the feather next to it.

Figure 5.23

Lay your feathers so that the tips of the feathers form a nice, round curve along the outer edge of your bustle. Once the outer edge is set, use a marker to draw a line along the base quills of the feathers, extension rods if you're using them, and cut them along that line. Before cutting the feather quills, number the feathers so you know their order throughout the rest of the project. If you're extending the feathers, secure your extension rod in place before laying the feathers in a circle and marking the place to cut the extension rod.

Once the feather quills are cut you can attach a loop using your preferred method. A stiff loop material is recommended to prevent the feathers from bunching up when strung together. Cover and decorate the base of the feather and extension rods. Remember to keep the feathers in order throughout the entire process. While a string through the end loops will keep the feathers in order, a bridle string holds the feathers neatly in place, layering them together like feathers on a wing. The leading edge of one feather should cover the trailing edge of the neighboring feather.

Figure 5.24 indicates the position of a bridle string. Carefully drill or burn a hole through the feather calamus or extension rod and run a bridle string from one feather to another. Beads between feathers work well as spacers to keep the feathers evenly spaced and can add aesthetic value when color coordinated with the base coverings and/or center rosette. Another method is to cut a slit in the ventral side of the rachis to pass a shoestring through as one does for bonnets.

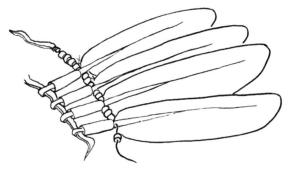

Figure 5.24 Sketch indicates the use of bridle string to set the feathers in order. Note the use of beads as spacers & as a design element.

When stringing bustle feathers together there are two common methods. Either string the feathers as one continuous ring of feathers like one does for a bonnet, or in two halves of the bustle, each side being like a set of wings. My preference is to do a continuous loop of feathers if using eagle tails but two halves if using primary spikes and secondary wing feathers. Making wing bustles in two halves allows the bustle to move more like the wings of a bird as the dancer soars around the arbor on the song.

Figure 5.25 Detail view of feathers strung together through self-loop & bridle string.

Bustle bases cut from thick leather make excellent foundations on which to build your bustle. Other materials can be used, e.g. plywood, particle board, and acrylic plastic, but these may require more specialized tools for cutting and drilling. Furthermore, rigid materials will be less comfortable to wear but the heavy leather will bend to the curve of the dancer's lower back and still remain firm enough to hold the feathers in place.

Figure 5.26 presents a diagram of a bustle base. This is a generic template and can be modified as needed to suit the specific characteristics of your bustle or to alter the presentation of the feathers.

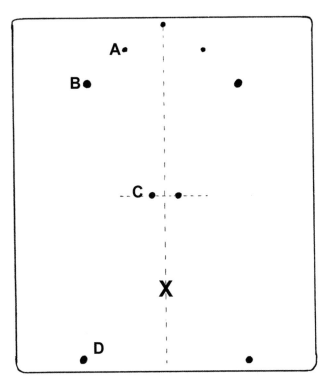

Figure 5.26

A – Holes for wire post to which the bridle strings are tied. 1/8" holes (4mm) Drill hole A one-fourth of the width from center line to edge and down from top edge halfway between the top and hole B.

B – Holes for the strings of feathers. Move holes farther apart for wing bustles to get U-shape from feathers. 1/4" hole (6mm) Drill hole one-third the distance from center to edge and one-quarter the distance from top edge to mid-line.

C – Center rosette placement. 1/8" holes (4mm) about 1/4" (1cm) from center line.

D – Attachment point for trailer(s). Move the holes closer to allow more swing of a single trailer. 1/4" hole (1cm) 1/4" up from bottom.

X – Hole placement if feathers are in two halves instead of a single section. 1/4" hole (6mm)

If adding an inner row of feathers to line the main bustle one will need another set of holes just to the inside of Holes-B. The beautiful bustle worn by John Butler on the back cover of The Northern Traditional Dancer contains a cluster rosette of eagle coverts. This style of inner feather decoration can be made more like the rings of an old-style bustle and held in place by the center rosette being tied in place and no further holes will be necessary in the leather base.

Figure 5.27 shows another view of the base with bent wire in place. Wire coat hanger works well for support and is easily bent with pliers. As indicated in the sketch, the top hole is for tying the bent wire in place with a little waxed cord. Use a pair of pliers to bend the wire over upon itself to form a loop. One can wrap the wire with colored electrical tape to decorate it to match the colors in the bustle. As the loop is formed, wrap the wire with tape to secure the end of the wire in place. The bridle strings can be tied directly to the wire loop or passed through these loops and tied together between them. Pulling the bridle string up tighter will lift the entire ring of feathers to project them out away from the wearer.

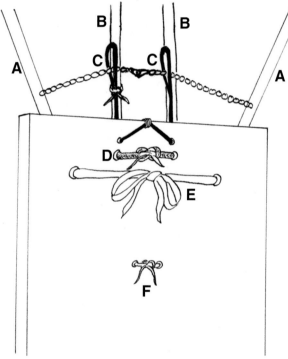

Figure 5.27

A – The first feather of the bustle

B – Upright spikes

C – Wire posts. Upright spikes are tied to the wire posts

D – Leather ties at base of the upright spikes tied at the back of the base.

E – Leather ties that string the bustle feathers together and tie at the back of the base.

F – Center rosette tied in place.

A quick and easy method for fastening the bridle strings between the uprights, or directly to the upright loop, is a fishing swivel. Secure the bridle string to the looped end of the swivel. The clasped ends will connect to each other directly between the uprights or to the loop in a pigtail wire (See **Figure 5.28**).

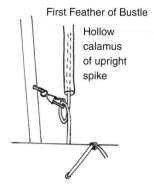

First Feather of Bustle

Hollow calamus of upright spike

Figure 5.28   Detail view of feathers strung together through self-loop & bridle string. : Pigtail loop in wire upright with swivel connected directly to the loop.

As the sketch in **Figure 5.28** indicates, the pigtail wire serves a dual purpose as connections for the bridle string and for placement of the upright spikes. Again, use pliers to bend the wire into a full loop about an inch and a half above the top of the base and leave a few inches of excess wire projecting upward. The hollow shaft of the spikes can slide down over this upright wire.

In the figure above, the upright spikes are shown attached to the base by way of a single leather thong wrapped to the base of the feather extension. Each leather strap is passed through additional holes drilled in the base and tied in the back. The extension is held in the upright position by tying it directly to the wire post.

Another fine example of a contemporary swing bustle is pictured to the left. This bustle employs a number of the techniques presented in previous chapters. The feathers are not a full set of matching wings but, rather, a conglomeration of miscellaneous feathers carefully selected and set in order to resemble wing sets. Each wing feather has had a primary covert feather affixed at the base. Though not shown in the photos, under-wing coverts were also attached on the back side of each feather.

Feathers of the main bustle are extended with a wooden dowel. Covering the extension rods are remnants of a Hudson's Bay 4-point blanket. The black, red and yellow colors derive from the stripes along either end of the blanket. The colors were chosen to match the corresponding feathers; black for wing feathers, red for tail feathers, yellow for the upright spikes. Each wool covering is sewn in using a whip stitch.

Feather plumes are wrapped onto the tips of each of the first three primary wing feathers while the remaining wing feathers have Angora goat hair glued on the tips. Both the feathers and the goat hair give life to the bustle as they sway and flutter with the movements of the dancer.

Hanging from the bottom of the base is a single, wide trailer of red wool approximately twelve inches wide by twenty-two inches long. Ribbon binding is stitched along the two side edges but the cloth is not backed with any other material. Three pairs of feathers are tied on the trailer, positioned in a triangle. At the base of each pair of feathers they are strung together with waxed thread and a pony bead spacer. White leather covers the lower section of the feathers and small fluffs are glued in place under the leather. White ermine strips decorate the tips of the feathers on the bustle trailer.

on as a backing with a plastic, butter dish lid providing some rigidity to the whole piece as an insert between the leather layers. Cobalt blue beads cover the stitching around the circumference of the centerpiece. Plastic lids may not be historically accurate or a 'traditional' material but it serves the purpose of keeping the piece rigid, which, in turn, holds the feathers in place instead of each half folding inward while dancing. Rawhide wasn't available to me at the time and, being hidden from view, doesn't detract from the aesthetic value of the bustle.

Figure 5.29 This bustle was photographed about 12 years ago and belonged to a Seneca friend of mine.

Figure 5.30 Detail view of inner area of bustle showing quilled rosette with feather attachments. Also shown are the bridle strings passed through the upright bases and tied to each other. Note the corresponding color scheme between the bustle feathers, wool base coverings and the quill rosette.

While we've seen thus far so much in the design scheme and execution of feather techniques for a visually striking bustle, the upright spikes are the dazzling focal point that brings the bustle to life. Not only are the colors and quill-work of the spikes more vibrant colors, but they are true works of art as they employ a number of feather techniques.

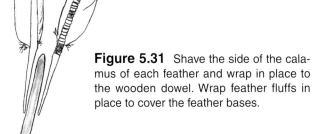

Figure 5.31 Shave the side of the calamus of each feather and wrap in place to the wooden dowel. Wrap feather fluffs in place to cover the feather bases.

At the center, a quilled and beaded rosette with feather dangles is secured in place. The quill-work is a series of concentric rings of quill-wrapped rawhide. Continuing with the color schemes of the bustle, black quills mirror the dark rays of the wing feathers while red reflects the tail section at the bottom. At the top, center, a yellow triangle mirrors the upright spikes jutting skyward. Each of the quilled concentric rings is stitched onto brain-tanned leather. Another piece of leather is stitched

To create the V-shape, the primary wing feathers are spliced back to back. This actually required four tenth position primary feathers which would mean two pair of wings would be needed. As this bustle was pieced together from miscellaneous feathers instead of full wing sets, it was a matter of careful selection to find the right feathers that could be spliced accordingly.

At the tip of the upright spikes the yellow fluffs are wrapped in place with waxed thread (see **Figure 5.32**). As **Figure 5.32** indicates these wrappings also work to hold the rawhide strip in place. Cut a thin strip on the end of the rawhide by removing thin sections from each side. The quilled strip is also wrapped into place at the base of the feathers as shown in **Figure 5.31** but it should also be tied in place along the length of the feather shaft. Thin strips of sinew can be passed between the feather vane barbs so the vane itself isn't disrupted much by these threads. As the sinew is translucent it blends well with the quillwork.

Figure 5.32

The bases of the upright spike extensions are covered with the Hudson's Bay blanket remnants just like the other feather extensions. Having been hollowed out, the extensions are slipped down over the wire uprights.

About halfway up the extension holes have been drilled through the extension to allow the bridle string of the bustle to pass. The bridle string attachment of this technique allows one to pull the feathers up tight to position the feathers higher and project outward from the dancer or to hang lower, thus allowing the feathers to sway more with the dancer's movements. This also holds the uprights securely as the weight of the feathers firmly sets the uprights on the vertical wire posts.

The yellow fluffs used on the upright spikes have been dyed in a bath of RIT dye. After rinsing and air drying on a paper towel they were re-fluffed with the help of a hair dryer.

Additional Tips and Techniques

The main feathers can be attached to the base by sliding the hollow feather quill or feather extension of the first feather down over a wire post.

For quick attachment of the bustle base to the belt rivet two-one inch wide belt clips to the

bustle base (available from Tandy leather). Slide the metal clips down over your heavy leather belt at the back for wearing. It just as quickly slides off without having to unbuckle your entire belt and side tabs when taking a break from a dance session.

If the feather halves of the bustle are closing in on themselves adjust the wire posts upright and farther apart. Using a larger centerpiece that is drawn up tight will also help prevent this.

When the bustle flattens, a.k.a. pancakes, adjust the wire posts to jut away from the body. Also, shorten the bridle string by removing beads between each feather. Shortening the bridle string also corrects the bustle shape when the feathers along the bottom of the bustle bunch up and fold over each other.

Figure 5.33

Pheasant Feather Bustle

Since its introduction to the U.S., the plumage of the Ring-necked pheasant has been an attraction to the Native Americans. Research indicates different dates of introduction of the pheasant to the U.S. from China, but one can generally deduce that pheasant feather bustles were not common among traditional dancers until 1915-1920. Nearly 100 years later these bustles are still popular and gaining in popularity with the resurgence of Chicken Dancers. The pheasant tail bustle can be used for an old-style outfit from the early 20th century or for chicken dance outfits with a contemporary flare. Basic construction is much like the old-style bustle with a leather base, trailer(s) and a feather wheel made of layers of concentric rings of feathers (see **Figure 5.34**) and cloth trailer. Pheasant bustles generally lack the characteristic upright spikes or tail section of old-style bustles.

Figure 5.34

A simple bustle can be assembled with about 100 tail feathers. That works out to be about 8-10 full tails and a couple wings. Naturally, more feather rings and more feathers per ring can be used as one desires. The use of wing feathers near the center adds bulk and variation in color and style to a pheasant bustle. Hen pheasant tail and wing feathers are good mimics of the Sage Grouse tail feathers that were employed in old style bustles across the plains and prairie. These birds are endemic to North America so their use in decoration pre-dates the use of pheasant feathers but their feathers are increasingly more difficult to acquire than pheasant.

Begin by sorting the feathers by size. The longest feathers will be in the outer rings progressing to shorter feathers near the center. Leather loops added to the base of each feather is a faster method than the self-looping as the pheasant calamus is much smaller and more difficult to self-loop. Cut a large amount of leather strips 1/8 inch (4mm) wide and 1.5 inches (3.5 cm) long. Pull apart lengths of imitation sinew into the thinnest threads possible to use in wrapping the leather loops in place.

While the prospect of looping, lacing and bridle stringing 150 feathers seems daunting, with a little practice one can finish all this in an afternoon. In the time it takes to watch a movie or two you can have all the feathers finished and set in concentric rings. One can strip and serrate feathers or decorate tips with fluffs as described in Chapter 3. Chicken Dancers seem especially fond of fluff-tipped pheasant feathers. The added weight of fluffs on the end of a long, delicate feather adds a unique flowing motion characteristic of pheasant tail feathers.

The use of a leather cone at the back of the feather cluster seems especially useful in pheasant bustles. Cut a round disc of three inches in diameter. Remove a wedge of leather from the outer edge to the center and stitch together the edges from where the wedge has been excised. This will create your cone.

Once again, the trailer can be either of one wide cloth or two, thinner strips depending on the dancers' preference. Attach the trailer by folding the cloth down and stitching to create a loop at one end. Run a dowel rod through the loop to hang the cloth and then tie the dowel to the bustle base. An excellent old-style look is the use of two wool strips with the full skin of a pheasant on each trailer. The brilliant plumage of a cock pheasant flashes with the movement of the dancer.

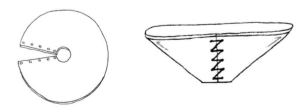

Figure 5.35

Contemporary Crow Bustle

Contemporary style Crow dance outfits, including the bustle, are a whole different breed of traditional dance. Anyone who has had the opportunity to experience Crow Fair has certainly witnessed the singular characteristics and unique style of the modern Crow traditional dancers. The beautiful design and style of the modern Crow outfit has certainly caught the eye of many a traditional dancer across the country. Traditional dancers in Crow attire can be found at just about every pow-wow from East coast to West. As such, I wanted to include a section on the construction techniques for the modern Crow bustle. Since my experience in creating this style of modern Crow bustle is limited I sought the advice of several experienced craftsmen. Thom Meyers of Buffalo Chips Indian Arts & Crafts has a lifetimes worth of experience with the Crow and generously shared his knowledge with me. Another friend was very helpful with information that he acquired directly from a member of a well respected Crow family at Crow Fair on the construction of the rooster coque bustle.

We're going to look at the construction of two different types of modern Crow bustles. The first is the 'fluff' bustle which consists mainly of colorful, T-base fluffs on the main body of the bustle as opposed to rooster tail feathers. These fluff bustles can be found in a wide range of pastel colors giving the appearance of wisps of cotton candy. The following instructions were described to me by Thom Meyers.

As with any project, one needs a firm foundation on which to build their latest masterpiece. This type of bustle base is a pillow of sorts. These bases have been seen in use on museum specimens of old-style bustles but are rarely seen in modern times except for this type of modern Crow bustle. Cut a strip of latigo leather or rawhide five by ten inches (13x26 cm) and fold in half to form a five inch by five inch square. Punch holes about one-half to three-quarters of an inch (2 cm) apart along the three open sides and sew the sides closed with imitation sinew. Before stitching the bottom, opposite the fold, stuff the base with whatever material you may have available, such as horsehair, buffalo wool, fur, leather scraps or cloth rags. Stitch the bottom closed through your pre-punched holes to finish your pillow base.

T-base fluff feathers that cover the front of your 5 x 5 base are strung in multiple, horizontal rows of strung feathers. There will be as many

horizontal rows of fluffs as there are holes along the edge. Each of the sample bustles I created when preparing to write this section of the book had five horizontal rows of T-base fluffs. Pass your thread through a hole on one edge of the pillow base and beginning threading as many fluffs on that thread as you can to span the five inch width of the base. I used four packages of 2 oounces of T-base fluffs and had some leftover for use on the upright spikes. After you've got your strand full of fluffs run the thread back through the hole opposite the hole you began with. Leave a tail of about eight inches on the back side of the base from the hole you began the strand and the hole you end each strand. Do not secure the threads just yet.

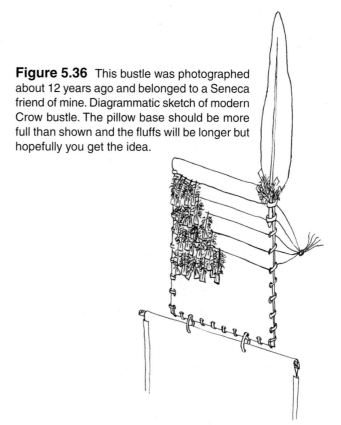

Figure 5.36 This bustle was photographed about 12 years ago and belonged to a Seneca friend of mine. Diagrammatic sketch of modern Crow bustle. The pillow base should be more full than shown and the fluffs will be longer but hopefully you get the idea.

Once you have all of the horizontal strands in place on the front side of the base, tie the tails of each strand together into one big knot on each side of the base. (See **Figure 5.36**) As these strands are knotted together on each side, tie them all together once again in the very center of the back of the bustle base. Pull these strands tight to snug the bases of the fluffs against the front of the pillow base and the fluffs will stand out away from you instead of laying flat against the base.

Prepare your upright spikes of primary feathers by securing some fluffs around the base with sinew wrappings. You can add some smaller fluffs to the tips as well. Set them in place with a little adhesive or a few wrappings of sinew. Attach your spikes to the bustle base by sewing them in place along each side. Use the same holes you punched for sewing the pillow together to lash the spikes in place. There's no particular way of doing it as long as they are held securely in place.

While talking with Thom about the Crow dancers and their traditions and such he informed me that the trailer of the Crow bustle should be of one piece of cloth. This rectangular trailer represents the encampment area of the united families of the Crow nation. Historically when the families came together they set up their camp in a rectangle or square field as opposed the traditional circular fashion of the Lakota nation. The single trailer is generally decorated with three horizontal rows of four or five feathers. Secondary or tertial feathers are more often employed than larger tail or wing feathers. The example bustle in **Figure 5.38** utilizes six small to medium wing feathers on the trailer.

Loop each feather and attach any adornments desired at the base of each feather. A small tuft of fluff to match your main bustle is nice but a contrasting color can also be rather eye catching. Use a thin strip of leather or sinew to tie each feather to the trailer.

Any cloth of heavy cotton, velveteen or wool in a dark color would make a fine trailer. Cut the cloth about ten inches wide. The length of the trailer will vary according to your height. Sewing a colorful ribbon binding along the sides and bottom makes a nice finished look. Fold over the top two inches of your trailer cloth and sew in place to make a loop along the top. Insert a wooden dowel or stick to hang your trailer. Attach the whole trailer assembly by lacing through the same holes you punched along the bottom of the pillow. (See **Figure 5.37**) Cut the dowel rod just short of the width of the trailer. Make a few stitches along each edge of the loop containing the dowel rod and you won't have to worry about it sliding out while you're dancing

Use a heavy leather thong to create loops on the back of the pillow base. Run the lace through several of the holes already in place and secure in place. On the sample bustle I made a couple x-cuts on the back and created shoestring loops. (See **Figure 5.37**) Run your belt or woven sash through these loops for wearing the bustle.

Thom pointed out to me that these bustles are not generally meant to be taken apart for travel and storage. As you see in **Figure 5.37**, the spikes and trailer are permanently attached to the pillow base. Carefully fold up the trailer and place the whole bustle in a box or small, hard-sided suitcase and you're ready to travel.

Figure 5.38
One of the author's modern Crow bustles completed using the directions presented here. It's simple but stylish and ready to dance.

Figure 5.37
Detail photo of the back of pillow base. Note shoestring loops for belt and trailer sewn along bottom.

Many modern Crow style bustles are made with the long, slender iridescent rooster coque feathers. The directions that follow focus on creating a rooster coque bustle. These bustles are a beautiful sight and the bundles of iridescent tails flutter and sway with the dancer's movements.

A base of rawhide or heavy leather folded in half and stitched along the bottom edge will provide the support you need. Carefully make T-cuts for inserting the upright spikes (see **Figure 5.15** of the Old-Style bustles section for alternative methods). Unlike the variety of fur-wrapped spikes on old-style bustles, the modern Crow usually has plain eagle primary wing feathers. Some of the examples seen at Crow Fair have fluffs added around the base and at the tip. If you choose to decorate the base and/or tips of your spikes keep it simple with a minimum of fluffs. The extravagantly dyed, stripped, parried and cut feathers are not as common in the modern style bustle.

One of the main characteristics of the modern Crow that distinguishes it from the old-style crow belt is the lack of a feather wheel. Instead of concentric rings of feathers centered on the front of the leather base, feathers are placed in horizontal rows of small bundles of feathers. The sketch to the right indicates the placement of feather bundles on the base. While doing some research on the modern Crow, friend Tom House told me that he has 81 bundles of feathers, nine rows of nine bundles. Lay out the 9x9 grid with a pencil and cut holes in place for each bundle. There are several ways to put together each feather bundle. Which method you choose may depend on what materials you have at your disposal and how much money you have to spend on materials, but whichever of the following methods you choose, your result should be a fine looking bustle.

The basic structure of each feather bundle is to secure a cluster of feathers around a short section of wooden dowel. Each dowel is then affixed to the leather base. The type of feathers used tends to change over the years just as any manner of fashion and fad also changes. Another friend and Crow style dancer has told me that some Crow dancers are now starting to use eagle body or tail covert feathers. Whatever it is you choose, be sure to purchase plenty of feathers to complete the entire project. As with any project you undertake, the first step is to gather all the materials you need before you begin.

Supply List

- heavy leather or rawhide, 20"x9" (51x23cm) fold in half for finished base of 9" wide by 10"
- 4 – 3/16" x 36" (1x91cm) wooden dowels.
- 80-90 small eye screws, 1/8" eye by 3/4" long (4mm x 1.5cm)
- 350 feathers, an approximation but this should be enough for the main body of the bustle and additions to the spikes. Coque & fluffs can be purchased in strands of feathers stitched together.
- 2 primary wing spikes, (1 right, 1 left)
- 6-8 wing feathers for trailer decoration
- 1/4 yd (0.25 m) cloth for trailer, solid color
- 2 yd (2 m) ribbon for edge of trailers (optional)
- imitation sinew or similar
- 1 skein of yarn
- glue

Figure 5.39
Simplified sketch showing parts of the modern, rooster coque Crow bustle.

Gather together your feathers, imitation sinew, dowels and glue. Smear a light layer of glue over half the length of the dowel. While holding a group of feathers in place with one hand, secure the feathers in place with a few tight wraps of waxed cord. (**Figure 5.40**) Experiment on a few dowels, without glue, to see what number of feathers will best fill the area around the dowel. Do your best to set the feathers such that the entire circumference of the wooden dowel is covered. Similarly, any areas not covered with feathers can be decorated by wrapping yarn or macramé cord over the waxed thread. Secure decorative thread with a bit of glue that dries clear.

Figure 5.40

A beautiful Northern Traditional bustle designed by Scott Evans and constructed entirely of hand-painted feathers by the late Joe Little.

A basic traditional bustle using the feathers from a pair of semi-mature wings.

Traditional dancer, Steve Charging Eagle, wearing a bustle of bald eagle tail feathers.
Photo by C. Scott Evans.

Mark Roanhorse wearing a fully beaded outfit with his bustle made of black & white feathers and carrying an eagle wing fan. Note the drop feathers on his hoop.

From left to right, John Butler, C. Scott Evans and Terry Larvie show the diversity of style as well as the coloration of feathers in traditional dance bustles while attending the Denver March Powwow. *Photo by Beverly Medhaug.*

A nice black and white traditional bustle being worn at the Stanford Powwow, circa 1990, at Palo Alto, California. *Photo by John Butler.*

Brooks Good Iron wearing a large black & white eagle bustle at the 1990 Rosebud Fair Powwow, Rosebud, S.D. *Photo by Art Gentry.*

When the glue used in securing the feather bundles has sufficiently cured cut the dowel off half and inch (1.5 cm) below the feather bundle. Screw an eye screw into the end of each of the feather bundle dowels as shown in the sketch to the left. You may need to pre-drill a tiny starter hole. A small drop of super glue in the pilot hole will help secure the eye screw so that it doesn't come unscrewed over years of dancing.

Make a series of holes in the rawhide base, with one hole for each feather bundle to be attached. Eighty-one holes in a nine hole by nine holes grid as shown in , previous page. Alternatively a drill will work well to make these holes through heavy latigo leather and rawhide. The hole should be just large enough to pass the eye screw through. Secure each bundle in place by running a leather lace through and around each eye screw. Run the lace through a hole in the base and pull taught before tying a knot to secure the line (see **Figure 5.41**). This line will allow the bundles a bit of movement to bounce and dance with the dancer while holding the bundles securely in place. One alternative would be to drill a smaller hole, one narrower than the eye itself, and screw each bundle in place directly to the rawhide base. Hold the bundle and dowel in position over the hole with one hand while screwing the eye screw through the rawhide base and into the dowel with the other. The small hole will open up a bit over time. In fact, the more you dance the faster it will stretch and allow more freedom of movement of the feather bundles. My friend who counseled me on modern Crow bustle construction commented that it may take a couple seasons of dancing before the feathers really begin to move well. So, the more you use your new bustle the better it looks.

Figure 5.41

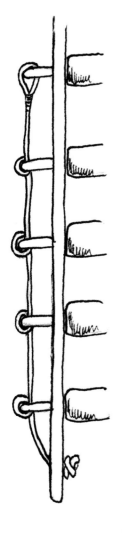

Once all the feather bundles are in place and secured, fold the leather base in half and stitch along the bottom. Prepare the spikes by adding a leather thong to the end of the primary wing feather. This lace can pass through the T-cut on the front and out a hole in the back side of the bustle base. Pull the laces snug to secure the spikes in an upright position and tie them together in a bow. You can loosen the laces and pull the spikes out of the base for travel. Feather fluffs added to the base or tip of the spikes can be wrapped in place with a bit of sinew and glue. Instead of removable spikes, you can also secure them along the side permanently as described previously in the directions for the 'fluff' bustle.

As I had mentioned earlier in this section of the chapter, Crow bustles traditionally have one, wide trailer but some contemporary dancers do employ a double trailer as shown in **Figure 5.13**. Fold over a two inch section on one end and stitch in place to create a loop. Insert a six inch section of dowel rod into this loop. A leather lace passed through the cloth and tied around the wooden dowel. Use this lace to tie the trailer to the bottom of the bustle base. After creating the loop at the top, sew a colored ribbon edge down each side of the trailer. This makes a nice clean look to the trailers. A ribbon color that matches the colorful feathers of the bustle helps develop an overall aesthetic appeal to the bustle. Trailers without edging are just as common as edged trailers.

Prepare each of the trailer feather decorations with the addition of the loop at the base. Both a self-loop of the calamus and an added leather loop work equally well so the choice is yours. Colored fluffs can be added to the base of each feather with a cloth or leather 'firecracker' to cover the base fluffs. Tie each feather individually to the trailer with a leather lace or imitation sinew.

Alternative Techniques

Instead of using wooden dowel rods as the base for each feather bundle you could use a spare feather calamus. Cut a two inch segment of feather quill from a scrap feather. Self-loop the base of it and secure with a dab of glue or sinew wrapping. Finish each bundle in the same manner as previously described, by wrapping the rooster coque around the circumference of the scrap calamus. There are a couple options for attaching bundles to the bustle base. You could pass the loop of each bundle through the leather base and secure on the inside with a leather lace through the row of loops in a similar fashion as described for securing eye screws. Instead of making holes for each bundle just cut an X and push the bundle through.

Rather than passing each bundle through the bustle base, you can use the loops of each bundle to string it on the front of the bustle base. Secure the lace on one side by knotting it through the base. String a number of bundles on the lace and secure again to the base on the other edge of the bustle base. When finished you will once again have multiple, horizontal rows of feather bundles on the front of the bustle base.

Instead of using an eye screw in each dowel you can drill a hole transversely through the dowel, below the feathers. String the dowels together on the surface of the bustle base as described above. This method will allow the feathers to move and bounce with the dancer and requires less material and hence less money invested if that is a concern for you.

Feather Clusters & Feather Wheels

Feather clusters can make an eye-catching addition to a dance outfit in a variety of ways: attached to the shoulder for traditional and grass dancers, armbands, shields, dance staffs, breastplates, bustle center-pieces, bustle trailers, roach pins, or anything else that comes to mind. The feather clusters add an additional degree of motion as the feather group flutters and sways in the slightest breeze.

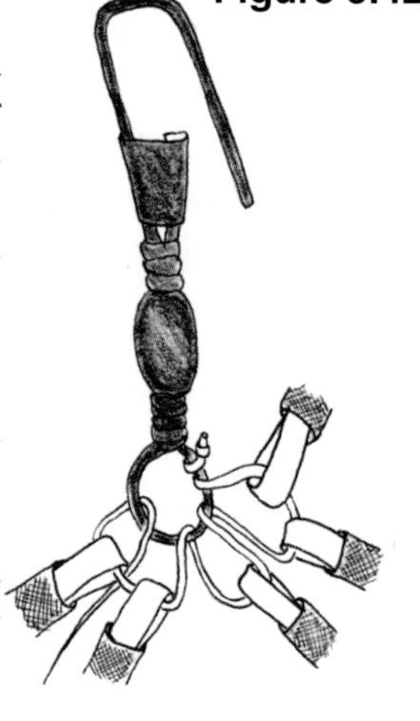

Figure 5.42

Figure 5.42 shows a simple method for creating these feather clusters. The use of fishing swivels makes for easy attachment/detachment on one's dance outfit and the swivel also allows for more movement of the feather cluster while dancing.

Begin with adding loops to the base of each of the feathers to be used in the cluster. Use imitation sinew to sew the looped feathers onto the circle end of the fishing swivel. One can add the feathers in a more random, hap-hazard fashion as shown as long as they are securely attached; but another method would be to add each feather in a similar fashion to tying bundles of hair for a roach. After securing the string with a knot on the ring pass the thread through a feather loop then complete a half-hitch around the ring. (As in Figure 5.42) After adding each feather, make a half-hitch around the ring. This will secure the feathers in a more uniform manner.

Gather together your feathers, imitation sinew, dowels and glue. Smear a light layer of glue over half the length of the dowel. While holding a group of feathers in place with one hand, secure the feathers in place with a few tight wraps of waxed cord. (**Figure 5.40**) Experiment on a few dowels, without glue, to see what number of feathers will best fill the area around the dowel. Do your best to set the feathers such that the entire circumference of the wooden dowel is covered. Similarly, any areas not covered with feathers can be decorated by wrapping yarn or macramé cord over the waxed thread. Secure decorative thread with a bit of glue that dries clear.

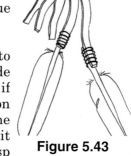

A simple addition to this technique can help hide the metal swivel from view if desired. Stitch a small section of leather in place around the barrel of the swivel and let it fold down over the spring clasp

Figure 5.43

end. This will discretely cover the swivel without hindering the spinning action.

My research has uncovered another method of creating what may be called a feather cluster or perhaps more aptly, a feather rosette. It is a technique that may well be described as nearly ancient, as museum examples date back to the early 19th century.

These wheels use the same construction techniques as tying bundles of porcupine hair for a roach. Crop a series of feathers short as illustrated in **Figure 5.44**, gleaning two short feathers from one, longer wing feather. Strip off the last one inch of vane from each side of the rachis. Carefully shave down the rachis with a sharp knife on this one inch section, keeping the dorsal side of the rachis intact. Using a heavy cotton or linen cord attached to a taught standing line;

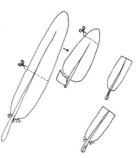

Figure 5.44

add individual feathers by bending the thinned rachis over the taught cord and tying the feather in place with a half-hitch around the bent rachis then around the standing line. See **Figure 5.45** above and right. Continue adding feathers in this fashion until you've reached your desired length of strand. The feathers in such strands were usually cropped straight along the tip.

A strand of feathers can be used to decorate the edge of a shield, strung along the length of dance staffs, wound around a staff to have the feath-

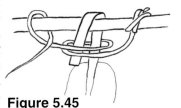

Figure 5.45

ers radiate outward, or used in different styles of bonnet. As **Figure 5.46** shows the completed strand can be coiled into a circle and attached as a feather wheel to a part of the dancer's outfit. These feather wheels were also once commonly worn as part of a man's wapegnaka or other hair ornament. Several museum examples of these cropped-feather, coiled strands have had the feathers dyed shades of red, orange and blue.

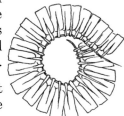

It should be noted that when coiled, the ventral side of the feather faces outward so as to be viewed by any onlook-

Figure 5.46

ers. **Figure 5.47** presents a feathered wheel of intricate design with a few simple techniques. The innermost row of feathers have been dyed, stripped, trimmed on the ends and set firmly in a manner so as to have them radiate outward from the center. The under-layers of feathers are white or dyed a light color to offset the dark feathers overlaid upon them and thus creating a dazzling design. The centerpiece can be a mirror, painted rawhide, a glimmering piece of costume jewelry, or whatever else one desires.

The use of positive and negative space in feather wheels can create eye-catching, mesmerizing works of art like the feather wheel shown here. The black feathers on top can be a separate wheel of feathers over the top of a light colored background. To better keep the trimmed

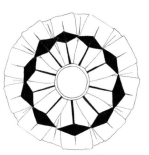

Figure 5.47

feathers in place over the background color, each of the trimmed feathers can be sewn, or hot glued, over the top of each background feather. Parry the ventral side of the rachis of the trimmed feather so it fits closer to the background feathers' rachis when set in place.

A simple and effective technique useful in creating a feather wheel that requires the feathers to maintain a set distance between them is the use of a heavy leather disk cut in the shape of a cog, or wheel with teeth. **Figure 5.48** illustrates the method of stringing the feathers between the teeth of the cog. Carefully burning a hole through the calamus tip with a hot needle or awl will help prevent the quill from splitting as you string them together. I use a large needle held by a hemostat or in vise grips. Heat it over a candle and poke the hot needle through the feather quill. Wear some sunglasses to help protect your eyes from the bright light of the candle flame.

A piece of thick packing tape around the calamus will also prevent splitting if you don't wish to burn holes in the feathers (it can be a bit smelly). Cut the tip of the calamus flat and set it close to the leather in the bottom of each 'pocket' as you string the feathers together. This prevents the feathers' rotating forward and back without the necessity of a bridle string.

Figure 5.48

Use an awl to punch holes transversely through each tooth/spoke in preparation for stringing the feathers in place with imitation sinew. Feather wheels of this design can be employed in feathered hair ornament, shield decorations, bustle construction, arm bustles, etc.

Preparing Roach Feathers

Figure 5.49 shows a simple yet secure method of attaching two feathers in a double socket roach spreader. As indicated, this method utilizes light chain segments to connect the two feathers. After cutting off the tip of the calamus, cut a notch in the calamus about an inch (2.5cm) up from the bottom.

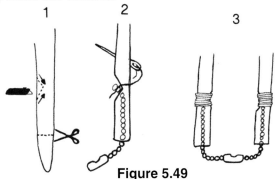

Figure 5.49

Tie a length of imitation sinew to the chain and thread the string up through the calamus and out through the notch. Wrap the string around the calamus and tie off to secure the chain within the feather. Make sure your chains are long enough to reach between the two sockets of your spreader. The chains will connect on the underside of the spreader and hold your feathers securely while allowing for lots of spinning action.

These chains can be purchased through many craft and hobby supply stores. They are inexpensive and the use of light chains can be useful in a multitude of ways when preparing your outfit so it doesn't hurt to keep a small stock in your craft toolbox.

Figure 5.50
This is one set of my roach feathers assembled in the manner as described previously. I've never had a roach feather fall out when dancing and these crest feathers move well in the sockets of the roach spreader.

Gustoweh

The traditional hat of the Eastern tribes like the Iroquois is called the Gustoweh.

Begin by making a frame for the skull cap. Latigo leather or rawhide will work well for giving the skull cap some shape instead of being too flimsy. A very traditional medium is basketry splints, often of ash. Most frame designs consist of a one inch wide strip that goes around the head with two, one inch wide strips that transverse up and over the crown of the head. **Figure 5.51** shows a finished frame and the points of stitching.

Before covering the framework, attach a center post on the very top. The feather clusters will be affixed around the top post and a single eagle feather can be held in place in the top post. The center post on top can be fashioned from any of a multitude of traditional and contemporary materials. A hollow bone from a deer or turkey leg is easily accessible and an easy medium with which to work. Cut the cleaned leg bone into a one and a half to two inch section. The top can be decorated with simple scrimshaw and carved designs using a dremel tool or left plain. Drill holes around the bottom for tying this piece into place at the apex of the crown frame. Imitation sinew works quite well for this step. Before tying the post into place, cut a

six inch length of wire coat hanger and, using needle-nosed pliers, bend a small loop at one end. When tying the center post into place, insert the wire into the hollow shaft of the bone section and pass the string through the loop. (**Figure 5.52**) This will secure the wire length in place at the same time of affixing the bone section to the framework. This wire piece will hold the center feather as the finishing touch to your Gustoweh.

Figure 5.51
Finished frame with antler piece attached at apex. Ready for sewing cover in place.

Figure 5.52

The frame is covered with velvet, velveteen, polyester, gabardine or wool cloth in dark hues of blue or green. Refer to **Figure 5.53** for a pattern of the cloth covering. Cut a rectangle of fabric in which the length (C) is one inch (2.5 cm) longer than the circumference of the leather brow band and the height (B) is equal to half the measure across the crown of the head from ear to ear plus three inches (7.5 cm). The V-cuts along the top edge will act as pleats for shortening the top edge as it puckers to the apex of the crown. Measurement A is approximately 4 inches (10 cm). Sew the points together by stitching edge 1 to edge 1, edge 2 to edge 2 and so forth. Each V-cut pleat can be sewn up using a running stitch or machine sewn before hand-sewing the fabric into place around the frame.

Figure 5.53

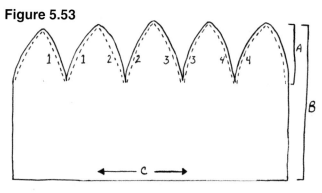

To finish the pucker and close the gap at the top of the head, run a single thread in a running stitch along the top edge. When you get back to where you began the stitch pull each end of the thread to tighten and pucker the top edge, cinching the fabric around the base of the center post. Tie the thread ends in a square knot. Refer to **Figure 5.54**.

Figure 5.54

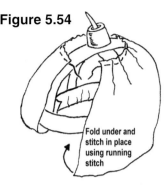

Fold under and stitch in place using running stitch

Along the bottom edge, fold the fabric over the brow band and sew the fabric with a running stitch along the inside of the hat. Use a thread that closely matches the fabric since the stitches will be visible; keeping the stitches smaller will help hide them as well.

Once you return to the back seam where you began, continue the running stitch up along the seam from the brow band to the apex.

With the crown finished you're ready to add a cluster of feather flurries at the base of the center post on top. A simple method of creating the feather cluster is to prepare your feathers by stripping the vanes and removing the rachis. Add a loop or create a self-loop on each feather. Tie the base string at the bottom of the post then slide on a series of feathers. With a fourteen inch length of string of feathers begin wrapping that string around the post. Secure by tying the string at the top of the post. Another method is to strip the vanes completely from the feather and tying these strips into bundles for attachment to the Gustoweh crown (see **Figure 5.55**). Sew several bundles of longer feather strips near the back of the crown and bundles of shorter length around the front of the crown.

Figure 5.55

It should be noted that the Eastern peoples often used turkey feathers. A Gustoweh of stripped turkey feathers should not be considered in any way inferior to one of stripped hawk feathers. Turkey feathers are easily obtained from craft supply stores, local poultry farms or friendly hunters. One word of caution when selecting

turkey feathers would be to choose the right sub-species of turkey feather. There are four sub-species of wild turkey found in different locations around the U.S., the Eastern, Osceola, Merriam's and Rio Grande. When gathering materials for this or any other project that employs turkey feathers choose feathers from the correct sub-species of turkey that is endemic to the region your outfit typifies.

Gustoweh often have a silver brow band. These finished pieces can be purchased from a variety of craft supply stores. These supply stores also carry a variety of silver brooches and washer rings for decorating the velvet portion of the cap. Abstract beadwork done in traditional Iroquois fashion would also be apropos. Keep in mind that such abstract beadwork designs would be done in white beads only.

Among the tribes of the Iroquois confederacy, there are distinguishing characteristics of the Gustoweh that identify the wearers' tribal affiliation. According to **Costumes of the Iroquois**, by R. Gabor, the Seneca used one upright feather on top; the Cayuga used one feather that hung down at an angle from the top; the Onondaga used to two feathers, one upright and one hanging loose; the Oneida used three feathers with two upright and one hanging down loose; the Mohawk used three upright feathers; and the Tuscarora had no upright feathers on top, only a bundle of stripped feathers. When more than one crown feather was used each feather had its own bone or wooden socket for placement. Also of note, the Onondaga and Mohawk did not cover the frames entirely as described previously, but wrapped strips of cloth or buckskin around the frame strips only. (Gabor, p. 2, 7)

Figure 5.56
Iroquois style Gustoweh made by the author.

Figure 5.57

     The Seneca skull cap shown above is reported as being found on the battlefield after the "Wyoming Massacre" in 1778. This was a significant event in the course of the American Revolutionary War in Northeast Pennsylvania.

     The quilled brow band is quite unique. Although standard zig-zag embroidery was used, the new quills are spliced into the work by inserting the point of the new quill into the hollow shaft of the existing quill.

Gustoweh in collection of the Luzerne County Historical Society, Wilkes-Barre, PA

Wing Fans

     Wing fans are more often the accoutrement of men dancers. Such fans are created from the primary feathers of the wing, what equates to the 'wrist' and 'hand' bones. (See wing diagram in Chapter 1) Goose and turkey wings are excellent substitutes for a raptor wing fan. They look nice and are relatively easy to obtain from local hunters. However, if you are set on having a raptor wing fan, there are some legal alternatives. This photo shows an eagle wing fan I created in my youth. With some guidance from Bob Laidig I was able to piece together a variety of natural Black Spanish Turkey and Canada Goose feathers to replicate an eagle wing. Bob generously provided a couple of his painted wing feathers as the final touch. What follows are examples of wing fans constructed from natural and reproduction feathers.

Figure 5.58

     The first series of photos present a hawk wing fan created from painted goose, turkey, and chicken feathers. Individual feathers are positioned and cemented in place in such a fashion that a wing is re-built.

Figure 5.59

     Step 1: Select, shape, trim and paint a series of primary wing feathers. Remember that raptors have emarginated primaries, which means the feathers have a notch on both the leading and trailing edge. Set them in order. A bridle string with bead spacers between the feathers will help set them at a proper distance. Epoxy the feathers in place before layering on covert feathers. Note: review the photos in the reference section which present raptor wing feathers to better understand the shape of each primary wing feather

Figure 5.60

     Step 2: Several types of covert feathers are trimmed, painted and set in place. The primary coverts are cut down from turkey feathers and painted. Chicken feathers were the right size for median and marginal coverts as well as several of the alular quills. Primary coverts can be individually attached to each primary remex or set as a group and placed en masse over the base of the primary remiges.

Figure 5.61
    Step 3: Underwing coverts are painted and set in place. Different size feathers come from the underwing coverts of chicken and goose. When setting feathers be careful not to get your adhesive on the feather vane. Place a dollop of glue in position so that the feather calamus alone is set in the adhesive.

Once this point was reached it was time to set the whole wing assembly into a handle. I purchased a prefabricated wing fan handle from one of my suppliers and made some modifications. I cut down the overall length of the handle and inlet one side with a Dremel tool to allow the fan to set down in the depression. (Remember to wear eye, ear, and airway protection) As the wing was set in place with epoxy I added a few more underwing coverts as a finishing touch of realism.

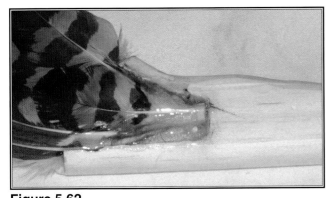

Figure 5.62
    Detail of hawk wing assembly inlayed in fan handle & glued in place.

When the epoxy was fully cured it had sunk into the hollow cavity. (**Figure 5.62**) Before wrapping any leather covering over the handle I filled the space with some air-dry, moldable clay. Auto body epoxy works well for this type of work as it too can be molded then sanded and painted after it dries.

While the previous wing fan set is a fun and interesting project to attempt, many dancers find the appeal of an eagle wing a bit more alluring.

The following directions for an eagle wing fan differ from what was given for the hawk wing fan set. I wanted to present this series of photos and instruction so that you can see how there is certainly more than one way to get the job done. Between each description and the additional tid-bits and tips included you should be able to put together an excellent wing fan for your next dance.

This faux eagle wing was created from all natural feathers that mimic the look of an immature Bald Eagle. The main primaries are from a Heritage Breed of turkey known as Sweetgrass with one hybrid turkey feather. Primary coverts were created from Black Spanish turkey wing coverts while the underwing coverts consist mainly of chicken secondary wing feathers and several crow feathers.

Figure 5.63
    Begin by selecting your primary feathers. An eagle has ten primary feathers but due to availability this fan will finish with eight. Note the sweeping curve that is distinctive of turkey primary remiges. Eagle primaries do not have such a curve so it is necessary to iron and shape them before proceeding. The rachis of a primary flight feather is much thicker so you will need to take more time in shaping. Begin heating the ventral side first to allow the feather to relax then continue shaping from the top side with your iron.

Figure 5.64
This photo shows the feathers after the initial shaping. Notice how the primary on the far left (primary #10) actually has a bit of a curve and is shorter than the other large, primary feathers. The feathers are arranged in the order they'll be in the fan set. (reminder, primaries are counted from the 'wrist' to the 'fingers' so that #10 is on the far left of this photo)

Figure 5.65
After the initial shaping I trimmed the feathers to give them the emarginated characteristic. This is a key factor in distinguishing raptor feathers from domestic fowl.

Notice how the 'notch' or 'shelf' of the trailing edge on the right moves farther out the shaft when progressing from primaries 9 through 4. Primaries 1-4 don't have a notch.

Figure 5.66
While the feathers from a mature turkey can be quite large, they still don't quite match the length of eagle feathers. Eagle wing primaries run about 18 to 20 inches (46-51 cm) in length and these large turkey feathers were only about 15 inches (38 cm) long.
These feathers were extended by inserting the quill from a scrap feather into the hollow calamus of my fan feather. A little bit of glue will generally hold it in place but this time I wanted to try the heat-shrink wrap. This tubing comes in varying sizes. I selected the half-inch tubing to allow plenty of room to slide over the joint. A little heat from a candle will shrink the tubing to a tight fit.

With the feathers shaped, trimmed and extended you're now ready to set them together. For the hawk wing set I simply applied a liberal amount of quick-dry epoxy while a piece of tape held the feathers in place. Turkey feathers are a bit too large for this and I wanted a better surface on which to place the subsequent covert feathers. I chose some air-drying modeling clay, Crayola brand, that is easily molded into any desired shape and is very lightweight when dried. Since this clay is made especially for children it can be found at many of the major craft supply warehouses as well as the ever popular department stores.

Figure 5.67

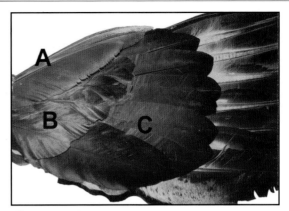

Figure 5.68 Detail view of coverts.
A – Alular quills
B – Marginal coverts
C – Primary coverts

After molding a piece of clay into a handle, insert each of your feathers so that they lay next to each other. The leading edge of a feather should overlap the trailing edge of the feather next to it. The clay dries slowly over the next 12-24 hours so you have time to manipulate the feathers into the shape you prefer. Some dancers like a wing fan that has the feathers more spread out so you can see some of the detail of each feather while others may prefer a 'closed' fan where the only feather you see in detail is the last primary feather. When piecing together a fan as shown here the closed wing fan can help hide the feathers, which, in turn, can add to the overall illusionary effect. Select feathers of the right color and set them to the proper length and half the illusion is finished because with the wing closed the overall appearance is that of a large wing which people will assume to be from an eagle. But don't let that be an excuse to cut corners.

Once the clay dries the primary coverts and alular quills are laid into place and secured with a quick-drying adhesive. I found special fabric glues especially useful as it was quick-setting but didn't bleed through the feather vanes to show on the front of the feather. The primary coverts are actually primary coverts but with a twist. These Black Spanish turkey feathers have iridescence on the leading edge, and came from the left wing. The wing being created is a right wing so I reshaped the primary coverts to look like right wing coverts and now the trailing edge of the feather becomes the leading edge, and lacks the iridescence.

You will need to carefully apply a bead of glue along the ventral rachis and set each feather in place as you layer the coverts. This is where the clay serves a great purpose. That clay handle isn't as much a handle for carrying the fan as it is a surface on which to build the remainder of the wing. It may be necessary to parry or carefully shave the ventral rachis thin as you layer one feather on top of another.

After placing each of the upper wing coverts in place and allowing sufficient drying time, flip the wing over and carefully place each individual underwing covert (see **Figure 5.69**).

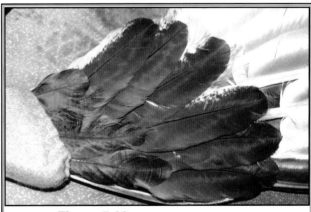

Figure 5.69
Detail view of underwing coverts.

Before layering on any of the coverts, I set a few small fluffs in place around the point of insertion of the feather extension rods in the clay and along each edge of the clay. These areas are mostly occluded by the coverts of course but the fluffs help to conceal the clay and the extension rods should someone take a really close look. Also, they tend to stick out from gaps between the coverts just like real down feathers on a bird.

Once completed the wing appears as though the coverts are just covering the lower portion of the primary feathers and their attachment point to the bones of the wing. With the fan set in the wooden handle it looks as though a wing, with bones intact, has been secured within a handle (**Figure 5.70** see next page).

Figure 5.70
Faux, immature Bald Eagle wing fan.

I formed this handle much as I did for the hawk wing set previously described. Beginning with a prefabricated wooden handle I trimmed some wood off and used a router bit in my dremel to inlet a section of the wood. In this space I fit the lower portion of the wing and secured it with several applications of epoxy. To cover and decorate the handle I stitched a Pendleton wool remnant in place that matches one of my traditional dance outfits.

Alternate Methods

Another good material for fan handles is Styrofoam. One can purchase blocks of Styrofoam at the major craft and florist supply stores. Instead of inserting flower stems make a nice feather fan arrangement by inserting your feather's quills. They'll hold in place well enough but it may be helpful to secure them with an adhesive once you've got them all set just as you desire. The Styrofoam can be easily cut and sanded to shape the handle as needed for both wing and flat fans.

I have described in Chapter 3 methods of splicing feathers in order to create a much larger feather that more closely resembles the size of an eagle feather. While I didn't do so for our turkey wing fan one could splice a section of feather vane to the extension piece in order to have a full length feather with full length vane to match. Real eagle wing primary spikes are about 18-20 inches (46-50 cm) in length with the vane running 16-17 inches (41-43 cm) along the rachis. This is just another of those added touches that may not be necessary but can result in a truly remarkable fan that closely resembles the real thing.

You can decorate your fan feathers once completed. Paint spots or apply colored tape on the tips, attach angora hair fluffs on the tip or a quilled rawhide strip along the rachis of each feather.

Small rhinestones glued in place on the tips of just the primary coverts with some diamond-cut pieces of reflective tape on the tips of the feathers would be dazzling to behold and certainly accentuate the movement of the fan while you are dancing. As I have said so many times before the possibilities are only limited by your creativity.

Tail Fans

Fan sets from the tail feathers of raptors are often carried by women dancers and men's Southern Straight dance. Throughout history there were times when both men's Fancy and Grass dancers carried tail fan sets and still today you may see some men's Traditional Dancers carrying one.

The process of transforming white, domestic turkey wing feathers into the tail feathers of a raptor takes much planning and research. As always, return to your reference photos to identify the key characteristics of each tail feather's three-dimensional shape. Feathers from the outer edge have a narrow leading edge and sharp curve in the rachis near the superior umbilicus while those nearer the center have vanes of equal width and no side-to-side curve of the rachis.

What follows in this section is a series of photos and instructions of the different stages of the process of tail fan set preparation. The first series of photos (**Figures 5.71 - 5.75**) is of a Red-tailed Hawk tail set. The second series of photos (**Figures 5.76 - 5.79**) is of a 7-feather, Sub-adult Golden Eagle tail set. Whether you're working on hawk or eagle tails the process is essentially the same; selecting good feathers, the initial shaping, painting, final shaping and trimming. That's a bit of an oversimplification but as I've mentioned before, the difference is in the details. So, read on to learn more about the details of the process.

Mesquakie Head & Tail Fan, ca. 1890 - Constructed from the head, skin and tail of an immature golden eagle, decorated with an appliqué beaded handle and three quill and horsehair feather shaft ornaments. *State Historical Society of Iowa, Iowa City. Photo 100204_1334.*

92

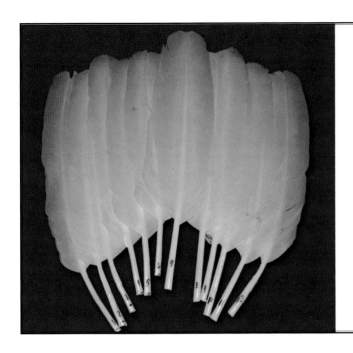

Figure 5.71

     Step 1: Select your prime feathers and prepare them for painting. Strip the lower rachis and crop to length. Shape the feathers by giving each rachis the proper curve based on the feathers' location in the tail set. Notice I've numbered each feather to keep them in order throughout the process.

Figure 5.72

     Step 2: Once your fan set is selected and pre-shaped you can go right on to painting the feathers. This image shows the painted feathers on the left while those on the right are on their way to the painting desk.

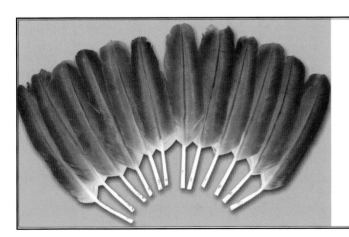

Figure 5.73

     Step 3: Finish with the painting of each feather. These feathers haven't had a final trimming and shaping

Figure 5.74

Step 4: The tail set is quite nearly finished after trimming each feather and giving the final shaping with a hot iron. Feathers on the outer edge have a thin leading edge with the leading edge widening as you move towards the center feathers. Final shaping also involves giving the feathers a slight front-to-back curve near the superior umbilicus. This mimics the aerodynamic shape of a raptor tail.

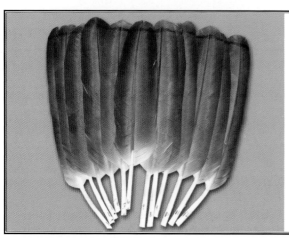

Figure 5.75

Step 5: The Final Touch: A black line is added to the tip of each feather. The overall shape of the set, after proper shaping and trimming, now resembles an actual tail as if just molted from a real bird.

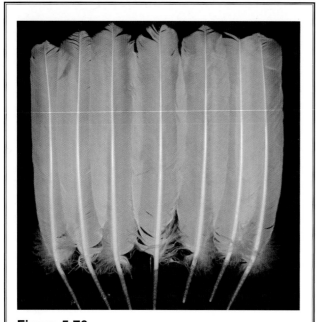

Figure 5.76

Feathers prepared for painting with initial shaping but not trimmed.

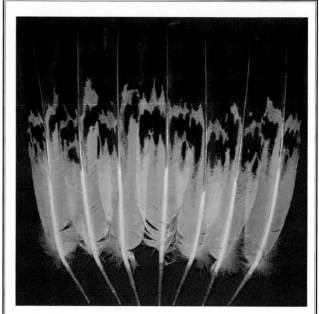

Figure 5.77

Feathers hand painted with brushes.

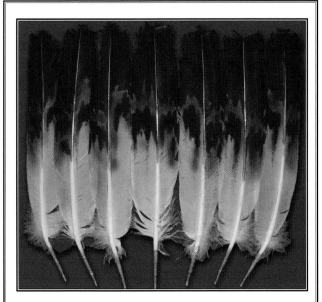

Figure 5.78

Painted feathers finished with an overspray for coloring & made off-white like eagle feathers.

Figure 5.79

Finished set of feathers after trimming.

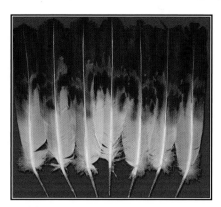

Figure 5.80

These feathers exhibit subtle differences from the last photo due to the final shaping of the feathers.

Presented below are a couple sketches to help illustrate the shape and layer of the tail feathers. **Figure 5.81** shows the side view of a raptor tail feather with characteristic 'hump' or curve near the superior umbilicus. This is also the form that you should be considering when creating single eagle tail feathers for roaches, bonnets, etc.

Figure 5.81

Figure 5.82 below indicates the manner in which tail feathers should be layered over each other when setting the feathers. This sketch shows the cross section view of the tail feathers with the leading edge of the feathers to the right and trailing edge to the left. Take note of how the leading edge of each feather curves slightly along the very edge of the leading vane. This closes the gap between each feather creating a perfect airfoil. When shaping your feathers and setting them in order for a fan set keep this in mind and review your reference photos often.

Figure 5.82

I would also like to make special note of the number of feathers in a tail fan set. Many people speak of 'center' tail feathers for roach feathers and fan sets but the fact is there is no center feather when there is an even number of feathers. Most raptors have twelve feathers in a full tail set, with a few hawk species having fourteen. Many wonderful fan sets are created with an odd number of feathers so as to have a center feather and I certainly wouldn't tell anyone they shouldn't do so. I only wish to mention that if you're creating a full tail set then make sure it has an even number of feathers, with no center feather.

The Kansa Indian delegation to Washington D.C., circa 1909 - 1910. Dressed in their finest regalia, the four men seated in front are carrying flat fans, two of which appear to be of the "head and tail" style popular during this period. *Glass Negative Photo*.

Frank Watson and Old Man Newally, Osage Straight Dancers carrying black and white eagle "head & tail" fans, photographed at Greyhorse, Oklahoma by Vince Dillon in 1912. *Glass Negative Photo*.

This young man appears to have been photographed prior to a dance, as he is wearing his roach and carrying a magnificent loose fan of black and white eagle tail feathers. *Photo courtesy of The Glass Negative*.

These photos illustrate the wide variety of feather types and coloration used in fan making, as well as a number of different loose and flat fan styles and variations. *Private collections*.

Mató-Tope, Mandan Chief
This portrait, painted by Karl Bodmer circa 1834, shows the chief dressed in his finest clothing and wearing his impressive eagle feather horned war bonnet, to which is attached a wooden replica of the knife he took from a Cheyenne warrior in hand to hand combat. He is carrying the special, feathered lance he used to kill the Arikara who slew his brother.
Lithograph courtesy of the Robert Wagner collection.

Chapter 6

Feather Use
in Historic Artifacts

While the majority of this text focuses on the usage of feathers in decorations and adornments that are generally in common use today, there remains a plethora of examples in museum collections of employing feathers and, indeed, whole bodies of birds in a variety of ways. Though these items aren't generally seen on modern dance outfits at pow-wows, they may just spark a bit of interest for the reproduction artisans or the craftsman looking to create something a little different.

When possible, I will provide some tips on construction of the artifacts included herein. However, as many of these items are stowed away in museum storage bins, actual construction techniques are not fully known. Presented are suggestions for how you might go about creating your own likeness of a historical piece. I will make every effort to note the museum location and catalog information of the specimens under discussion to facilitate your research should you choose to further investigate a particular item. Refer to the Appendix for a list of museum websites with searchable databases where the images of the items presented in this chapter can be found. In lieu of color images, I have provided several sketches of items based on their color photos available online.

Feathered Bags & Pouches

Native peoples have the reputation for not wasting anything, being resourceful and thrifty with those resources. The creation of bird skin bags, in all their forms, certainly seems to lend credence to this reputation.

The example presented here (Figure 6.1) is of an eagle leg skin bag in the collection of the American Museum of Natural History (AMNH). [50.1/5916] This bag possesses quillwork of extraordinary design and composition that certainly deserves more attention than what is given herein. However, as our focus is on feathers, we move our attention to that material employed in the bag's construction. This particular piece is made from the lower leg skin of a Golden Eagle. Being a booted eagle, the Golden Eagle provides more feathered skin to be used in such a fashion. It appears that the skin has been laid flat as decoration for the front piece with brain-tanned hide for the backing, as opposed to the leg section being stripped in a tubular or cased manner from the leg to create a pouch.

A variety of other feathered pouches, bags and pockets are found in museum collections. Most of these are from Indigenous peoples of the Arctic and utilize waterfowl bird skins like eider, duck, cormorant and loon. A list of several other items in the collection follows to facilitate the reader's own research.

Specimens in the AMNH include:
50/3925: Bag, loon skin. McKenzie River, Canada.
50/3931: Bag, loon skin. McKenzie River, Canada.
50.1/7665: Bag, Loon skin. Beaver;
Alberta, Canada.
50.2/2762: Pouch, Tobacco. Montagnais, Naskapi;
Newfoundland/Labrador, Canada.
50.2/627: Tobacco pouch, Loon skin. Montagnais, Escoumains/Tadousac; Canada.
50.2/2762: Pouch, Loon skin. Montagnais, Naskapi. Canada.
60/3481: Pouch, loon skin. Eskimo;
Point Barrow, Alaska
60/6815: Bird skin pouch. Eskimo, Alaska.
60.1/5440: Pocket, loon skin. Eskimo, Canada.
60.1/5451: Pocket, eider skin. Eskimo, Canada.

A number of birds, whose skins are available for legal purchase or procurement by hunting, could be used to make one's own bird-skin bag. The Ring-necked Pheasant (Phaesianus colchicus) cock is one such bird. Whole, salted skins can be purchased or fresh ones can be hunted up in many states. From a fresh hide, flesh the skin as clean as possible to remove all fat and sinews around the feather tips in the skin. Once fleshed, wash the hide with warm, soapy water to clean the blood and grease from the hide and feathers then rinse well with clean water. Taxidermists rinse bird skins in Coleman fuel to draw out the water and grease from a hide. Dunk the bird skin in the Coleman fuel and swish carefully to cover the entire hide. If you attempt this procedure take all necessary safety cautions. Wear protective eyewear, a heavy plastic apron, thick rubber gloves and an industrial

Figure 6.1
Golden Eagle Leg skin bag, decorated with porcupine quillwork, tin cones, red horsehair tassels and claws. *American Museum of Natural History No. 50.1/5916.*

mask to protect from the fumes. Perform this procedure outdoors in a well ventilated area. Tack the hide out on a board with pushpins and rub the flesh side with borax or immediately tumble the hide to dry. Bird skins can be dried well by tumbling them in a bag of corncob grit purchased from taxidermy supply stores. The grit dries the feathers as well as the skin. No special tanning solutions are necessary for bird skins as long as one has fleshed the hide thoroughly and dried it well.Cut a section from the dried hide to be used for decoration on your bag. Use a cloth backing to protect the bird skin with a whipstitch along the edges of the cloth and skin. Sew a section of leather to the bird skin along three sides leaving the top open. Sew these pieces inside out and turn them right-side out when finished. Cut the leather back longer so the top section can be folded over the opening as a closure flap to your pouch. Attach a simple leather thong to the back of the bag.

Medicine Pouches

The term of medicine bundle or medicine pouch is vague at best. My interpretation of medicine, for the purposes of this writing, is simply any materials of particular value to the possessor, either in spiritual or nostalgic context. As such, the idea of medicine pouches or bags is interpreted as a container for the safe-keeping of such items of value. These containers may be the property of an individual person or of a society at large. When used by a society the term bundle seems to be consistently used by scholars as it generally refers to a larger collection of items that are the paraphernalia that identify that society.

With our focus firmly set on feathers, we need not look far to find medicine pouches and bundles that are made from the skins of birds. **Figure 6.2** presents one such example. Many others like it can be found in the collection of the AMNH in which the entire skins of birds are used for storing precious items. Not all of these are lined with cloth but a few are.

Medicine bundles of bird skins in the collection of the AMNH:
50.1/9668: Bald Eagle bundle. Pawnee, Chaui.
50.2/203AB: Screech Owl. Pawnee, Chaui.
50.1/8424: Evening Star Bundle, stuffed bird skin. Pawnee.
50.1/8425: Evening Star Bundle, stuffed goose skin. Pawnee.

Figure 6.2
Golden Eagle medicine bundle of the Chaui Pawnee. The eagle skin is lined with cloth. *American Museum of Natural History Photograph No. 50.2/379.*

50.1/8430AB: Evening Star Bundle, stuffed Great Horned Owl. Pawnee.
50.1/9691: Duck head. Pawnee, Kitkahaxki.
50.1/9704AB: Hawk skin. Pawnee, Kitkahaxki.
50.1/9705AB: Hawk skin. Pawnee, Kitkahaxki.
50.2/2323: Mountain bluebird. Navajo.
50.2/2324: Lewis woodpecker. Navajo.
50.19967D: Shitepoke skin. Shoshoni.

Feathered Necklaces & Scarves

Necklaces of feathers on a twisted thong as well as whole body skins are found as parts of dance society regalia and in ceremonial usage. Kroeber describes several feathered necklaces associated with the Ghost Dance movement among the Arapaho in the *Anthropological Papers of the American Museum of Natural History*, Volume 18, part 4, 1907. Several examples consist of individual feathers attached to a length of twisted cord or hide. One Arapaho example is of braided rawhide dyed half red and half green with the feathers dyed as such to match the corresponding cordage. [AMNH 50/408, Kroeber, vol. 18, part 4, p. 338] Several other examples of this twisted or braided cordage necklace exist in the AMNH collection but perhaps the most unique is artifact 50/118, labeled Crow Dance Belt. [Kroeber, vol. 18, part 4, p. 339] This Arapaho piece is more likely worn as a scarf or necklace than as a belt around the waist. It is a light blue, silk scarf with silver brocade design. The scarf has been folded in half and along the two edges are a variety of sage grouse1, erroneously identified as pheasant feathers in volume 18, part 4, owl, magpie, and crow feathers. Most of these feathers have been dyed red with white fluffs or fur at the base. Several other items in the collection are labeled as belts but appear to have the same or similar construction techniques as other items identified as necklaces or scarves. Considering this similarity and the fact that they appear more like necklaces than the traditional 'crow belt' or bustle styles, I have chosen to include them in this list of feathered necklaces.

Specimens in the AMNH include:

50.1/9226: Shalako Feather Collar, Zuni.
50.1/9225: Sallimopuja Dance Collar, Zuni.
50/40: Waist Band, Arapaho. Kroeber, vol. 18, part 4, p. 338.
50/121A: Crow Belt Necklace, Arapaho.
50/408: Feathered Necklace Scarf, Arapaho. Kroeber, vol. 18, part 4, p. 338.
50.92A: Twisted Cord Feather Necklace, Arapaho. Kroeber, vol. 18, part 4, p. 337.
50/118: Silk Scarf Necklace/Crow Dance Belt, Arapaho. Kroeber, vol. 18, part 4, p. 339.
50/100: Crow Dance Necklace, Arapaho. Kroeber, vol. 18, part 4, p. 338.
50/330: Rabbit Foot and Feather Necklace, Arapaho. Kroeber, vol. 18, part 4, p. 339.
50/324: Feather Necklace, Arapaho. Kroeber, vol. 18, part 4, p. 337.1
50/3189: Feathered Shoulder Sash, Shasta. Dixon, vol. 17.
50.1/379: War Bundle Feather Strips, Ojibwa.

While the feather necklaces previously described are often associated with ceremonial or society regalia, there are other examples of feathered collars that are noted in the social dances of the late 19th and early 20th centuries. Several photographs from that era show Grass/Omaha Dancers wearing full bird skin necklaces. **Figure 6.3** presents an example of a full, crow skin necklace/choker. The full skins of birds worn as necklaces may have had their origins as society paraphernalia like that of the Crow Owners (Kangi yuha) Society among the Lakota. A Hunkpapa man by the name of Eagle Shield, 2Eagle Shield acted as informant to Francis Densmore in "Teton Sioux Music", Bulletin of American Ethnology, Bulletin 61, 1918. was photographed wearing a crow-skin necklace like that illustrated in **Figure 6.2**. [Frank Fiske, c.1918] This photo was reprinted in Teton Sioux Music, plate 40. Members of Big Foot's Band were photographed wearing bird-skin chokers as part of their dance regalia by Grabill around 1880. Similarly, Sioux Chief Little Eagle is wearing a bird-skin choker on an early 20th century postcard (photographer unknown).

Figure 6.3
Full crow skin choker identified in Bureau of American Ethnology Annual Bulletin, vol. 61, plate 44 as Crow Skin Necklace. This item is identified by Eagle Shield as an emblem of membership to Kangi'yuha society.

Other bird skin necklaces in the collections of the AMNH include:

50.1/5859L: War Bundle Hawk Skin Necklace, Menominee. (See sketch, **Figure 6.4**)
50.1/6369: War Dance Neck Ring, Wichita.

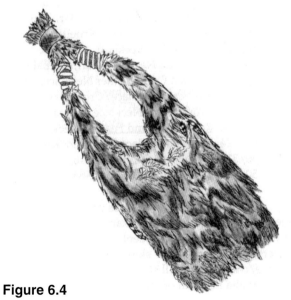

Figure 6.4
AMNH 50.1/5859 L Complete hawk skin cape. Red wool is wrapped around the end to hold the flaps together. Red wool wrappings are held in place with leather lace, presumably for comfort measures when wearing the hide around the neck. The description of this item identifies it as a War Bundle, Hawk Skin Necklace; Menominee.

Figure 6.5
AMNH 16.1/48 Cloak, Eagle Skin; North American Ethnographic Collection, *American Museum of Natural History.*

Blankets and Capes

Anyone who has slept soundly under the warmth of a down comforter knows well the insulating power of feathers. While the buffalo robe embodies the mystique of Native American culture and history, the buffalo isn't endemic to all parts of North America. Birds, however, of all shapes and sizes, are found from the artic tundra to the deciduous forests of the southern United States. Not only were birds an abundant resource, they certainly loomed large in the religious and spiritual beliefs of native peoples, thus making them even more desirable as decoration.

A cloak made of animal hide and the entire body skin of a mature Bald Eagle would seem to fit into the category of possessing spiritual significance to the artisan and wearer. **Figure 6.5** is a photograph of this cloak of the Okanagon people.

This eagle skin cape may be a one-of-a-kind piece but the author has found a poncho of similar design in that it has the entire skins of birds attached to it. The poncho is in the collection of the Peabody Museum of Harvard University [15-36-10/86604] and comes from the Thompson River region of the Canadian rockies. One hide of deer or elk is folded in half with a hole in the center to allow the wearer to pass his head through. Each half of the hide covers the front and back of the wearer. On each half of the poncho is the skin of a Great Horned Owl, sans skull. The head skin is positioned at the top near the neck line with tail and legs extending down below the bottom edge of the hide. The wings are spread out to either side of the body. Unfortunately no information is available as to the usage of this remarkable piece, whether for daily use in inclement weather or as a ceremonial garment.

My research has uncovered several other blankets noted as being made of eagle feathers. These however seem to be made of sections of skin sewn together in quilt-like fashion and containing all downy feathers as opposed to fully developed body feathers. Some of the tribes of the Arctic regions used the downy-covered chicks of Eider ducks as they were a relatively easy resource to acquire. An individual could walk through a nesting site where the Eider nests and chicks were on the ground and collect a meal as well as other material resources. This seems a bit more unlikely with the eagle down robes so perhaps it is more likely that the body feathers were plucked from the skin for use on other projects. Sections of downy-covered skin that remained were employed in creating a blanket.

Feathered blanket specimens in museum collections:

AMNH:
60.1/3897: Bird skin and fur. Eskimo of Prince of Wales, Alaska.
60.2/5343: Bird skin robe. Eskimo of Greenland.
16.1/1693: Down Blanket, possibly Tlingit. Alaska.
1/6750: Coat or Robe, bird skin in checker pattern. Possibly Tlingit. Alaska.
16.1/48: Cloak, Bald Eagle skin and hide. Okanagon. (see **Figure 6.5** for sketch)
60.1/5622: Cloak, winter Eider and Auk. Eskimo of Greenland.
E/2298: Eagle skin robe, downy. Tlingit.
60.1/6672: Eider skin pillows. Eskimo of Greenland.
60.1/7025ABC: Eider chick skins. Eskimo.
60.1/7114: Eider skin blanket. Eskimo.
60.1/5491: Eider skin robe. Eskimo.
60.2/5343: Eider skin robe. Eskimo of Greenland.
50.1/7889: Feather Blanket. Northern California.
16.1/1643: Down Feather Robe. Tlingit. Alaska.
60.1/7108: Feather Robe. Eskimo of Greenland.

Peabody Museum, Harvard University:
17-13-10/87052: Eider Down Blanket.
13-23-10/84680: Feather blanket. Maidu.
27-15-10/98238: Feather blanket. Maidu.
27-15-10/98240: Feather blanket. Maidu.

From the collections list it is clear that the use of whole skins for blankets was a common practice among the peoples of the north. These were not just items of functionality either. The details of design in patching together contrasting colors of bird skins are dazzling to behold.

Feather Clothing

Throughout the vast and vapid northern regions of the Arctic there exist few resources for survival. As a matter of necessity, the indigenous peoples became adept at utilizing any and all materials present. Bird skins were pieced together for parkas and outer boot covers when furs were not readily available.

The method of preparation of bird skins for use in making boots and parkas is described in *Our Boots; An Inuit Women's Art*. (Oakes & Riewe, 1995. p. 47) Eiders are skinned by beginning at the head and pulling the skin off toward the tail. This turns the skin inside out as a tube. Loose pieces of meat and fat can be scraped off, but to get the fat completely out of the skin (waterfowl are notoriously greasy) a much more aggressive technique must be undertaken. The skins are sucked clean of fat. There is some skill to be developed as sucking too strong will pull feathers through the skin, causing a chocking hazard, and not sucking hard enough will not only fail to remove the fat deposits but it will only result in making the hide water-soaked with saliva. When completed the flesh should be clean of all fat and nearly completely dry. Silatik Meeko, an artisan interviewed for *Our Boots*, noted that it takes about two hours of sucking to clean one skin (p. 47) One adult eider skin is generally enough for one boot. Details on the methods of construction of such boots can be found on page 72 of *Our Boots*. As described therein, it takes very little stitching to fashion a cleaned bird skin into a boot, with the finished product generally having the feathers on the outside. A pair of Eider skin boot covers can be seen on Plate 127 (page 132).

Two striking bird-skin parkas are shown in Plate 111 (page 118) of Our Boots. One is more akin to those of the AMNH collection with the feathers facing out and the colorful plumage adding a degree of aesthetic value to the functionality of the garment. The other parka has the feathers inward towards the wearer. While the skin coloration of the parka is not as visually appealing, what catches the eye of any onlooker is the traditional cut and design of the parka. It possesses long lobes extending below the waist to the knees in front and back with an oversized hood. This style tends to be associated with the traditional women's garments of caribou fur and dates back several centuries. A garment of such style loses nothing in aesthetic value with the feathers hidden inside the parka.

Various feather garment specimens in museum collections include:

1/2307 A: Eider Skin Coat. Eskimo, Alaska. [AMNH]
60.1/8954: Duck skin parka. Eskimo, Nome, Alaska. [AMNH]
60/3479: Bird skin (Guillemot) Coat. Eskimo, St. Lawrence Island. [AMNH]
973-3-10/52081: Bird skin parka. Eskimo. [Peabody Museum]
69-30-10/2092: Coat of bird skins. Aleut. [Peabody Museum]
88-51-10/49956: Loon Skin Parka. [Peabody Museum]
91-16-60/51603: Bird skin coat. Ainu. [Peabody Museum]

Also discovered through research are two hats of particular interest. Each utilizes bird parts as decoration of the hats as opposed to being crafted from the body skins of the birds. A specimen in the Peabody Museum comes from the Thompson River region of Canada. [15-36-10/86603] The main cap is fashioned of tanned buckskin with ermine pelt and fur strips for side drops. Attached along either side of the hat and jutting directly back away from the head are the primary wings of a mature Golden Eagle. The main feathers with their primary coverts still attached are flared wide giving the impression of Mercury himself.

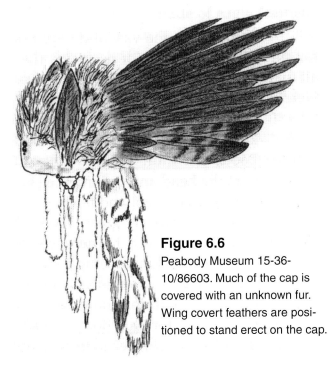

Figure 6.6
Peabody Museum 15-36-10/86603. Much of the cap is covered with an unknown fur. Wing covert feathers are positioned to stand erect on the cap.

The more striking of the two hats is a Crow hat in the collection of the Buffalo Bill Historical Center's (BBHC) Plains Indian Museum. [NA.203.168] To a cap of buffalo hide with the fur on are attached the wings and head of a golden eagle. Along each side of the head are attached the primary feathers of the wings, still attached to the bones and hide and so including the marginal covert feathers of the wing. At the apex of the cap is attached the stuffed head of the Golden Eagle, with brass buttons for eyes. A short section of the back skin and feathers flows from the eagle's head down the back of the cap. No beaded brow band exists on this hat but brass hawk bells are attached along the front edge of the cap.

In contrast to the use of assembled parts for decoration of hats, an item in the collection of the Peabody Museum that comes from the Arctic Regions of the far north is made from the entire skin of a loon. [07-47-10/72350] Specific construction details are uncertain. From the color image available from the online database it appears as though one skin has been used for the cap in much the same manner as one bird skin is used for each boot cover as described previously. It takes but a little imagination to envision the process of converting a clean Eider skin into a hat by cutting a line along the center of the pelt from neck to tail. As it is turned right-side out again the edges of this incision will become the bottom edge of the cap as it encircles the head. It is unknown if the cap is lined with cloth. A liner may make it more comfortable for wear but is certainly not a necessity.

Shield Decorations

While there exist in museum and private collections shields adorned with a plethora of feathers attached around the perimeter, on cloth streamers or at various loci in feather clusters, shields with full bird bodies attached are particularly striking. As shields are often a representation of very personal beliefs of the owner it can be deduced that the choice of bird skin decorating the shield also had some very personal meaning. Any discussion beyond that as to the meaning of the birds would be mere conjecture.

A shield in the Cody Museum has the entire skin of a male Kestrel (Falco sparverius) attached to the front. The main body has been skinned of flesh but the skull is still intact. The wings are spread out to either side with the tail hanging down. A color photo of this shield appears in *Pocket Guide to Native Americans, page 49. (Westhorp & Collins, 1993)*

Sioux War Shield
This shield is painted in eight alternating sections of red and yellow, with four bear paws painted in black. Further decorations include four eagle wing feathers with mottled coloring and six long narrow feathers, possibly seagull feathers bundled together and tied in the center of the shield.
BAE Bulletin 61, Plate 48.

Several shields have the heads only of the Sandhill Crane (Grus canadensis) attached. The crane may be considered by some a rather mundane bird but it is indeed remarkable in action and character in possession of a subtle, but indefatigable beauty. Sandhill crane plumage is generally a dun gray with a bright red crown atop its head. A shield in the Fenn Collection [FCSHIE76] has a bird head that appears similar to the Sandhill Crane in that it has a long, slender beak of a water bird. I think it is more likely a Great Egret (Ardea alba). This shield was owned by Thunder Bear, an Oglala Lakota man of Pine Ridge, South Dakota. Photographer Richard Throssel photographed a Crow man, Shot In The Head, carrying a shield with a Canada Goose (Branta canadensis) head attached to the front. Actually, this particular shield is not just the stuffed head but also has the tail clump attached and two clusters of goose wing feathers on either side of the goose's neck. The head and neck are stuffed with buffalo hair to give it lifelike, three-dimensionality.

A shield in the AMNH [50.2/4800] has the entire skin of a Great Horned Owl (Bubo virginianis). This piece is not spread out in the fashion of the Kestrel previously described but wrapped in some cotton cloth wound around the main body from neck to the base of the tail and attached in the center of the shield. Another whole bird example in the AMNH collection is less prominent. It isn't a great 'bird of thunder' on the front of the shield but the delicate little body of a song bird. This shield is identified as Wolf-lies-down's by Robert Lowie in the Anthropological Papers of the AMNH, volume 25, part 2. While this shield is depicted in a sketch it is not described in detail to identify the bird or give account for its use on this particular shield. (Lowie, v25, part 2. Figure 4, page 405).

The Peabody Museum of Harvard University has several excellent shields in their collection. One in particular has the head of a Prairie Falcon (Falco mexicanus) with skull intact and wing segments attached. [05-7-10/64948] This isn't quite the full body but more a style of abstract art with the parts affixed in a manner to make it look like an entire body is attached.

Of similar design, that is, using the parts of the body to make the appearance of a full body of a bird of prey, is a shield in the Carnegie Museum of Natural History [24118-119] which has the head and tail of a hawk along with a selection of primary wing feathers arrayed on the shield. A sketch of this shield is shown in **Figure 6.7**.

Figure 6.7
War Shield in the Carnegie Museum of Natural History. Parts of the hawk are arranged on the shield to give the abstract appearance of the body of the hawk. *Author's sketch.*

Rattles

Rawhide rattles are a common item used in both social and ceremonial events. While the method of manufacture of rattles varies from region to region, the use of feathers for decoration of the rattles is quite consistent. **Figure 6.8** depicts one of the more common styles of rattle with cropped feathers along its seam.

Figure 6.8
Heavily decorated with feathers, this Cheyenne Crazy Dog Society Rattle, is in the collection of the *American Museum of Natural History. 50/5514.*

As depicted in the sketch, the feather adornments of rattles are generally attached along the upper edge of the rattle, away from the handle section. One museum specimen has the skin of a Western Screech Owl (Otus kennicottii) wrapped over the handle section. [AMNH 50/354] This singular piece is described by Kroeber in "The Arapaho, Religion" as representing the entire body of a man. 4 Anthropological Papers of the AMNH, vol. 18, part 4. Figure 178, pp 445-446. A bulbous head on the rattle is the head of the man with feathers and bells as hair ornament. Painted portions of the rattle symbolize such elements as the sun, a rainbow and sun-rays. The owl skin is of great significance in the use of this rattle. As the Screech Owls are thought to be ghosts, this rattle is used to frighten away ghosts.

Not all rattles were used in ceremony or for healing. Some were used in social dances just as in Gourd Dancing at today's pow-wows.

Museum specimens of rattles with feather adornment:

08-4-10/72802: Cheyenne Rattle. Peabody Museum.
985-27-10/60160: Dance Rattle, Arapaho. Peabody Museum.
985-27-10/59495: Ponca Rattle. Peabody Museum
50.1/4333: Horse Society Rattle, Mandan. AMNH
50.1/4343: Kit Fox Society Rattle, Mandan or Hidatsa. AMNH
50/4478: Rattle, Blackfeet or Peigan. AMNH
50/6844: Rattle, Crow. AMNH
50.1/9651: Rattle, Pawnee. AMNH
50/1806: Star Dance Rattle, Gros Ventre. AMNH
50/1783: Star Dance Rattle, Gros Ventre. AMNH
50/1808: Star Dance Rattle, Gros Ventre. AMNH
50/1767: Star Dance Rattle, Gros Ventre. AMNH

Horned Bonnet

Many students of the material culture of the Native Peoples of North America may be familiar with the variety of split-horned bonnets. Many of these head dresses have coverings of ermine fur strips but there are a number of same that employ short, cropped feathers in transverse rows across the crown of the cap. A bonnet identified as Buffalo Dance headdress of the Mandan or Hidatsa has black feathers cut to about two to three inches in length. [87-11-10/40898] These short feathers are attached to the apex of the cap between the horns which rise up from either side of the head. This technique is also employed on the Strong Heart Society (a.k.a. No Flight Society) bonnet that is an insignia of membership in this prestigious Lakota society. Beuchel Museum online database presents a record of such a bonnet, BMLM Number 0132. See also Densmore, *"Teton Sioux Music,"* p. 320 and *Wissler, "Societies and Ceremonial Associations of the Oglala,"* p. 25. Wissler refers to this society as The Braves.

Other uses of feathers in the production of the split-horned bonnet are shown in **Figure 6.9**. Feather clusters dangling from the tips of the horns is common. A little less common is the wrapping of the horn tip with bird skin in colorful plumage. The iridescent green crown of the Ring-necked Pheasant or that of any of a variety of similarly hued waterfowl feathers serve well as decoration.

Figure 6.9
Author's example of feather adornment of split-horned bonnet horns.

Split-horned bonnets in museum collections that accentuate feather decorations:

NA.205.78: Sioux Buffalo Horn Bonnet,
BBHC – PIM
NA.203.18: Buffalo Horn & Owl feather bonnet,
Crow. BBHC-PIM.

985-27-10/60275: Bison horn cap.
Peabody Museum.
40-39-10/19383: Sioux Bonnet. Peabody Museum.
50.1/1267: Medicine Bonnet, Cheyenne. AMNH.
50/8435: War Bonnet, Jicarilla Apache. AMNH.
50/8304: War Bonnet, Mescalero Apache. AMNH.
50.2/5113: War Bonnet, Arapaho. AMNH.
50/8496: War Bonnet, Jicarilla Apache. AMNH.
50.1/393: War Bonnet, Lower Brule Sioux.
Whole hawk skin on cap. AMNH

Appendix

Appendix A: Taxonomic Classification of Raptors (from Manual of Ornithology)
Domain – Eukaryota
Kingdom – Animalia
Phylum – Chordata
Class – Aves
    Subclass - Neornithes
    Superorder – Neognathea
Order – Falconiformes
Family – Accipitridae
    Subfamily – Pandioninae: Osprey
    Accipitrinae: Hawks, eagles, accipiters, kites

Appendix B: Bird of Prey List (Raptors of North America, Snyder)

Vultures
    California Condor (Gynmogyps californianus)
      Turkey vulture (Cathartes aura)
      Black Vulture (Coragyps atratus)

Kites
    White-tailed kite (Elanus leucurus)
    Everglade (Snail) Kite (Rostrhamus sociabilis)
    Hook-billed kite (Chondrohierax uncinatus)
    Mexico and Central America
    Mississippi kite (Ictinia mississippiensis)
    Swallow-tailed Kite (Elanoides forficatus)

Harriers
  Northern Harrier (Circus cyaneus)

Accipiter Hawks
    Northern Goshawk (Accipiter gentilis)
    Cooper's Hawk (Accipiter cooperii)
    Sharp-shinned Hawk (Accipiter striatus)

Buteo Hawks
    Broad-winged Hawk (Buteo platypterus)
    Red-tailed Hawk (Buteo jamaicensis)
    Red-shouldered Hawk (Buteo lineatus)
    Gray Hawk (Asturina nitida) Mainly Mexico.
    Short-tailed Hawk (Buteo brachyurus)
    Swainson's Hawk (Buteo swainsoni)
    Rough-legged Hawk (Buteo lagopus)
    Ferruginous Hawk (Buteo regalis)
    White-tailed hawk (Buteo albicaudatus)
    Zone-tailed Hawk (Buteo albanotatus)
    Common Black Hawk (Buteogallus anthracinus)
    Bay-winged (Harris's) Hawk (Parabuteo unicinctus)

Ospreys
    Osprey (Pandion haliaetus)

Eagles
    Golden Eagle (Aquila chrysaetos)
    Bald Eagle (Haliaeetus leucocephalus)

Falcons and Caracaras
    Gyrfalcon (Falco rusticolus)
    Peregrine Falcon (Falco peregrinus)
    Prairie Falcon (Falco mexicanus)
    Aplomodo Falcon (Falco femoralis) Mexico
    Merlin (Falco columbarius)
    American Kestrel (Falco sparverius)
    Crested Caracara (Caracara cheriway)

Barn Owls
   Barn Owl (Tyto alba)

Eagle, Snowy, Wood, Eared and Screech Owls
   Great Horned Owl (Bubo virginianus)
   Snowy Owl (Nyctea scandiaca)
   Great Grey Owl (Strix nebulosa)
   Barred Owl (Strix varia)
   Spotted Owl (Strix occidentalis)
   Short-eared Owl (Asio flammeus)
   Long-eared Owl (Asio otus)
   Eastern Screech Owl (Otus asio)
   Western Screech Owl (Otus kennicottii)
   Whiskered Screech Owl (Otus trichopsis)
   Flammulated Owl (Otus flammeolus)
Burrowing, Boreal, Saw-whet, Hawk, Pygmy, and
Elf Owls
Burrowing Owl
   (Athene cunicularia or Speotyto cunicularia)
   Boreal Owl (Aegolius funereus)
   Northern Saw-whet Owl (Aegolius acadicus)
   Northern Hawk Owl (Surnia ulula)
   Northern Pygmy Owl (Glaucidium gnoma)
   Ferruginous Pygmy Owl
   (Glaucidium brasilianum)
   Elf Owl (Micrathene whitneyi)

Appendix C: Non-Raptor species whose feathers
and parts were used in Native American feather
craft. This is a list of the more commonly found
birds in the prairie and plateau regions. Many
more birds were used but it is not possible to list
the names of every species of bird ever used in a
Native American artifact.

Names and information recovered from Cornell
Lab of Ornithology; All About Birds website.
*http://www.birds.cornell.edu/AllAboutBirds/Bi
rdGuide/* Retrieved February 12, 2008
   Greater Sage Grouse–Centrocercus urophasianus
   Gunnison Sage Grouse - Centrocercus minimus
   Greater Prairie Chicken – Tympanuchus cupido
   Lesser Prairie Chicken - Tympanuchus pallidicinctus
   Sharp-tailed Grouse - Tympanuchus phasianellus
   Ring-necked Pheasant - Phasianus colchicus
   Sandhill Crane - Grus canadensis
   Canada Goose – Branta Canadensis
   Tundra Swan - Cygnus columbianus
   Anhinga – Anhinga anhinga
   Northern Flicker, both yellow and red-shafted
   varieties - Colaptes auratus
   Black-billed Magpie - Pica hudsonia
   American Crow - Corvus brachyrhynchos
   Common Raven - Corvus corax

Appendix D: Federal Migratory Bird Laws and
Treaties.

   The laws that regulate the possession,
sale or barter of raptor feathers are too lengthy
to include in their entirety. Everyone should fa-
miliarize themselves with these laws before
working with any feathers in their craftwork. Ig-
norance of the law isn't a substantial defense. I
am no lawyer so the information presented herein
is not for legal advice but for your reference.

   U.S. Code of Federal Regulation Title 50,
Part 22 (50CFR 22) states that "[T]he import, ex-
port, purchase, sale, trade, or barter of bald and
golden eagles, or their parts, nests, or eggs is pro-
hibited."
(*http://edocket.access.gpo.gov/cfr_2004/oc-
tqtr/pdf/50cfr22.1.pdf*) Exceptions to this law are
few, mainly for the "religious purposes of American
Indian tribes." (Ibid) To be able to claim the use of
feathers for religious purposes one must prove affiliation with a federally recognized tribe, i.e. a
tribal enrollment card.
   While this notes some of the restrictions on
eagle feathers, it should be mentioned that such restrictions also apply to many other birds that fall
under the protection of the Migratory Bird Treaty
Act. Web addresses are provided below to facilitate
your research efforts.

   U.S. Code of Federal Regulations. Title 50
– Wildlife and Fisheries. Chapter 1 – U.S. Fish
and Wildlife Services, Dept. of the Interior (cont.),
Part 22 – Eagle permits.
*http://www.access.gpo.gov/nara/cfr/waisidx_0
4/50cfr22_04.html*
   Birds Protected by the Migratory Bird
Treaty Act; List of Migratory Birds that fall under
the protection of the migratory treaty act. Included
in this list are the Bald and Golden Eagle.
*http://www.fws.gov/migratorybirds/intrnltr/m
bta/mbtandx.html*
   Birds Protected by the Migratory Bird
Treaty Act; Game Birds & Hunted Species. This list
represents birds that may be listed as a game
species by some states' wildlife departments. If a
game species, one may legally possess the feathers
and parts of the birds legally obtained according to
the hunting laws of that state but the sale, trade,
and/or barter of the bird or parts thereof may be restricted. *http://www.fws.gov/migratorybirds/in-
trnltr/mbta/gmebrd.html*
-      Bald Eagle Protection Act, enacted in 1940
with amendments in 1959, 1962, 1972, and 1978.
http://ipl.unm.edu/cwl/fedbook/eagleact.html
Retrieved April 20, 2008

Bibliography

Alsop III, Fred J. *Smithsonian Handbooks: Birds of the Mid-Atlantic.* New York, DK Publishing, Inc., 2002.

Bates, Craig D. "An Arapaho Bustle," *Moccasin Tracks*, Vol. 10, No. 4. (1984).

Brewer, Bill and Kathy. "Seventh Annual Howe Northern Dance," Event Program. 1987.

Densmore, Frances. "Chippewa Music II," Smithsonian Institution, Bureau of American Ethnology *Bulletin 53*. 1913.

_____. "Teton Sioux Music," Smithsonian Institution, Bureau of American Ethnology *Bulletin 61*. 1918.

Evans, C. Scott. *The Northern Traditional Dancer, 2nd Edition*. Pottsboro, Texas, Crazy Crow Trading Post. 1990.

Finster, Dave. "An Omaha Heduska Outfit," *American Indian Crafts & Culture*, Vol. 4, No. 9. (1970).

Fletcher, Alice C., and Francis LaFleche. "The Omaha Tribe," Smithsonian Institution, Bureau of American Ethnology *Twenty-seventh Annual Report*, 1905-1906. 1911.

Gabor, R. *Costumes of the Iroquois*. Ed. By Wm. Guy Spittal. Ontario, Canada. Iroqrafts, Inc. 2001.

"Gustoweh Headdress Kit Instructions," Carver, Massachusetts. Wandering Bull. 1999.

Hewitt, Rick. "A Northern Cheyenne Bustle," *Moccasin Tracks*, Vol. 12, No. 1. (1987).

Howard, James H. "Firecloud's Omaha or Grass Dance Costume, Part 2," *American Indian Crafts & Culture*, Vol. 6, No. 3. (1972).

Johnson, Michael. "A Canadian 'Crow Belt'," *American Indian Crafts & Culture*, Vol. 7, No. 3. (1973).

Jones, Craig. "Contest Fans," *Whispering Wind Magazine*, Vol. 36, No. 2. (2007).

Jull, Louie. "Traditional Style Crow Bustle," *American Indian Crafts & Culture*, Vol. 4, No. 5. (1970).

Kroeber, Alfred L. "The Arapaho, Part IV: Religion," American Museum of Natural History *Bulletin of the AMNH*, Vol. 18, Article 4. (1907).

John Butler, Sac & Fox

This Northern Traditional bustle, is made primarily of nicely matched, mature golden eagle tail feathers with mottled coloring. The trailers are decorated with black & white tail feathers and the extra center rosette of smaller wing feathers is interchangeable with another bustle. *Photo courtesy of John Butler.*

About the Author

My interest in Native American history, culture and especially material culture began in my youth. I was an active member of the Boy Scouts of America and The Order of the Arrow, an affiliate of the Boy Scouts. I worked at the local scout camp teaching various craft-working merit badges. It was during my youth when I came to know Bob Laidig as a friend and mentor. Bob gave a presentation to our local O.A. lodge that fueled my desire to learn more. He kindly took the time to teach me a great deal about craftwork and specifically instilled in me a passion for feather craft. A number of evenings were spent working one-on-one discussing the process of painting raptor feathers, the uses of natural mimics, and the multitude of reproduction projects that incorporate feathers.

My study of and participation in native culture has continued throughout my life. In 1998 I moved to Mission, South Dakota, the heart of the Rosebud Reservation, to teach science at the Todd County High School and to continue my education in Lakota life and culture. I spent six years on the Rosebud. I not only learned a great deal and improved my skills as a craftsman but I also spent my last year at T.C.H.S. co-teaching the Traditional Lakota Arts class. The course was based on a curriculum I had written the year before after I had discovered a need for students to learn some of the historical aspects of the material culture. During this time, I was creating more items than ever before and took some of my own work to a whole new level in order to show the students some new possibilities for their work.

Although I worked on painting faux raptor feathers in my youth, it wasn't until I was living in South Dakota that I began in earnest to develop my own dyes and produce some reproduction feathers for sale. After moving back to Pennsylvania in 2004, I officially started my business, Sioux Specialties, and began marketing my feathers and other reproduction items. While painting feathers is a main focus of my business, the impetus for producing top-quality feathers is the reproduction of historic artifacts. I enjoy using the feathers I create in a variety of projects and it's exciting to see how others use them in their own craftwork, as well. This was part of the reason I wanted to put together this book, to help others focus on feathers as part of their craftwork. The use of feathers as an art medium is an exciting venture that I enjoy sharing with others.